MENDING HEARTS, MENDING LIVES

Anne Pierson

Destiny Image Publishers
P.O. Box 351
Shippensburg, PA 17257

MENDING HEARTS, MENDING LIVES
Unless indicated otherwise, all Scripture references are taken from the New American Standard Bible.

ISBN 0-914903-30-6   Printed in the U.S.A.

Destiny Image Publishers
P.O. Box 351
Shippensburg, PA 17257

For Worldwide Distribution

To my parents
who taught me that
Jesus is the Great Restorer
and that caring
is more important than getting.

With Special Recognition
to my husband, Jim, who has been
the best father I have ever known to our children
and the children God has brought to us.
to our daughters, Holly and Shelly,
who have shared their lives,
their rooms,
their possessions,
and their parents.
to all the young women
we have been allowed to love.
Thank you.

TABLE OF CONTENTS

1

The Call

House a person in need? A pregnant woman? I couldn't! I'm not a nurse, I don't know anything about women in crisis pregnancy, and after all, I have small children. How would this influence the lives of my children?   These questions and more went through my mind as we took the first person into our home in 1972. She was an unwed, pregnant woman. As time went on, we took in runaways, people released from psychiatric hospitals, drug addicts, and many other women in crisis pregnancy.

My husband, Jim, myself, my grandpa, and our two daughters, nine-year-old Holly and six-year-old Shelly, were comfortably settled in our small, suburban Maryland home just outside Washington, D.C. We liked our life. Jim was a truck driver for a Baltimore firm, and I was a part-time secretary at the Library of Congress. Although I was a pastor's daughter, Jim and I had only within the past few years rededicated our lives to the Lord, and were now leading a non-denominational youth group in my father's church. I was the organizer, and Jim was the lover. The young people ate up the attention and affection he showered on them at each meeting. I have always appreciated that quality in Jim.

We were serving the Lord, we were raising two lovely daughters, we were giving grandpa a home, and between Jim's driving and my part-time work, we were making ends meet. What more could we want, or could the Lord expect from us?

It was about this time that Mary walked into our lives. She was brought to our youth group meeting by a friend: pregnant, alone, and very scared about what the future held for her. She didn't speak much during the meeting, but afterward she lingered with her friend long after the rest of the young people went home.

Neither Jim nor I knew what to say to her, or how to start. Finally, I brilliantly observed, "You're pregnant, aren't you?"

Her story came out slowly. She was in her first year of college and had become pregnant from a boy she didn't know very well. He was no longer in the picture. Mary had made an appointment for an abortion, but she couldn't go through with it. Going home was not an option as far as Mary was concerned. She had contacted a local maternity home where she could go to have her baby. But she wasn't looking forward to going to the large, "rather cold" (as she described it) institution. She had dropped out of school, and until it was time to go to the home, she was hiding herself in the college apartment with friends supplying her needs.

During her story, Jim and I looked at each other from across the room. We both knew what we had to do without even discussing it. Before she had finished her story, I offered our home to her for the remainder of her pregnancy.

That was our modest beginning. Mary accepted our invitation and came to live with us. As we walked through her pregnancy and the birth of her adorable son with her, we felt compassion for all the pregnant women we saw in the clinic. After talking with the counselor assigned to Mary from the adoption agency, we became aware of the massive extent of the problem of teen-age pregnancy.

It was the eve of the landmark abortion decision. Mary could have obtained an abortion easily, even though it would not have been legal to do so for another year. We knew nothing about abortion, and really did not want to get involved, and yet through this one person coming into our lives, everything had changed. We not only wanted to help Mary, but we felt impelled to help others like her.

We saw Mary blossom in our home. I noticed how well she related to Jim, and vice versa. She participated as a member of our family: in household chores, in devotions and church attendance, in helping with our children. "Lord," Jim and I would pray, "what this country needs is Christian families who will care for these young women in single families or small group homes. Please raise up your people to care enough to do this."

He did. Us! By mid-1973 we had sold everything we owned in Washington, packed up Holly, Shelly, Mary, and Grandpa, and purchased a seventeen-acre farm in rural Pennsylvania which would become home to us for the next eleven years. The House of His Creation, a home where young women could live and be shown the love of Jesus in a Christian family, was born.

Since making that commitment to extended family living, we have lived with over 200 young women. One of the many things Jim and I have learned is that there are two essential ingredients for those involved in this work — caring and loving. If we do not have these two vital ingredients, our service will be meaningless.

It is easy to read the Bible and even to think that something should be done to help wounded and hurting people. It is another thing to make the Scriptures live through us. C. T. Studd made a statement that I found worth remembering and have tried to incorporate into my life: "Some wish to live within the sound of chapel bells. I wish to run a rescue mission within a yard of hell."

3

As I considered C.T. Studd's statement, I realized a call of God to this work.

I have found that those who serve successfully in this important ministry do so out of a motivation of mercy first, rather than a motivation of salvation, sacrifice, or social justice.

A salvation motivation is necessary for some types of ministry. It is essential for those in the pastorate, those called to street ministry, or those in the mission field. Salvation is certainly something we desire for one and all, and most assuredly we desire it for the women who come to live with us. Our main motivation, however, for opening our homes to women in crisis pregnancy is mercy.

Mercy involves meeting someone's basic needs, as Jesus outlined in the judgment parable in Matthew 25: "I was hungry and you gave me something to eat; I was thirsty and you gave me drink, I was a stranger and you invited me in, naked and you clothed me, I was sick and you visited me, I was in prison and you came to me."

Young women who need housing have many of these needs. They need shelter and food, they need to learn basic life skills, they need to have love shown to them through our life examples. Through this, salvation is often realized, but when salvation is our primary motivation, we become frustrated and disillusioned very quickly. Some who come to us will have salvation experiences; others will leave us with no apparent spiritual changes. Occasionally we are called to be harvesters, but more often we are to be seed-planters.

One of the young women who came to live with us accepted Jesus in her first week in our home and has continued to walk with Him. On the other hand, we have had young women who have left us and have married and been divorced, and a few have even gone to prison. We are still trusting that the harvest will come for them.

4

Over the years we have found that approximately six out of ten young women with whom we've shared our lives have experienced real change. Lynn, is one whose life was changed. We received her through a detention center in another state. She was fifteen, pregnant, and charged with being "uncontrollable". Her parents loved her and loved God, and yet she had rebelled. She had been running away for some time. During one of these escapades, she became pregnant. The state officials had been involved in her case for some time and they were baffled by her case. She refused an abortion.

A Christian judge was hearing her case and our lives were drawn together through a series of circumstances. The end result of the court hearing was that Lynn would come and live with us (as her legal guardians) until she reached the age of eighteen!

The first months were difficult. She was not interested in "religion" in any form and fought anything that had to do with God. But because our motivation was mercy, we simply released our difficulties in this area to the Lord and worked on other challenges in her life.

After about a year with us, she did come to know Jesus through the many activities she and we were involved in (youth group, church, devotions at home). She went on to college, has led a youth group of her own, and is now happily married. Mercy motivated us, salvation joined hands with mercy, and she was made whole.

Another motivation to consider is sacrifice. We must make sure that we are not in this ministry because we are trying to make this "our big one for God." The corollary to this approach is: Certainly now God will love me, answer my prayers, and make sure I get to heaven."

It is true that the promises of God became more alive in our lives as we reach out to the poor and needy, but this, like salvation, must never be our main motivation. God will not honor our ministry when this is our motive.

Finally, one should *not* enter this ministry as a result of the motivation of social justice alone. At a pro-life meeting in Michigan I heard Russell Proctor make an important statement regarding this issue: "Do you love justice and do mercy, or do you love mercy and do justice?"

When justice is our motivation, the young women we serve see through this and we never accomplish all that we could with them. In working with a young woman in crisis pregnancy, justice usually shows itself through our concern for their unborn children. If your main motivation for taking a young woman into your home is to save her unborn child, she will begin to see herself only as a means to your end, and see you as someone who cares more about her baby than about her. Remember, when our main concern is the young woman, we also save the baby. Then we truly love mercy and do justice.

When we commit ourselves to extended family living we are committing ourselves to the battlefield. We are committing ourselves to teaching our children that actions speak much louder than words. We are saying to the world that we not only care but that we are willing to reach out with our lives and our families.

Jim and I have found three things to be critical to our ministry and to our own personal lives in order to maintain the right attitudes necessary to live as an extended family:

1) Being in the Word daily — the bible *must* be our manual for life. We must read and reread the principles that are so important to the raising of children, to our marriage, and to the many other parts of our lives. I started by reading a verse a day and now I am committed to reading the Bible through each year. Start somewhere, but *start*. I found that

6

once I became disciplined in this area, I yearned for more and more.

2) Having a quiet time. The results will be miraculous. I personally like to write out my prayer requests and record my answers. In 1986 I wrote out eighty-four specific prayer requests and by the year's end I had seen fifty-nine definite answers the these prayers.

Another part of my quiet time is to keep a thank you card to the Lord. Each month I begin a new card. During my quiet time each day I reflect back on the previous day and write down all the things I have to be thankful for. I believe our attitude toward each day is very much affected by our gratitude. When I am discouraged I often flip through my list of answered prayers and thank you cards.

3) Fellowship with other believers. We realized some time ago that if we were going to serve in this type of ministry, we needed to be going to a church that preached the Word and that supported our ministry. You need to be fed as well as to feed.

There are numerous Scriptures regarding our attitude toward the poor and needy. When Jim and I first entered this ministry, we needed to know that there was a real biblical basis for our giving not only our lives, but our children's lives in this way. We found that the Scriptures are full of instructions as to how we are to treat the poor and needy.

First of all, who are the poor and needy? Certainly, they may be people who are lacking material possessions. But being needy simply means to be in want. People who feel small in worth, or people who arouse pity in us are also needy. A person can be in want materially, physically, emotionally, or spiritually.

There are many Scriptures relating to this, but let me share two that warn us against denying the cry of the poor.

"He who gives to the poor will never want. But he who shuts his eyes will have many curses" (Prov. 28:27).

"He who shuts his ear to the cry of the poor will also cry himself and not be answered"(Prov. 21:13).

I certainly do not want to be found in the group of people described in these verses! I want my prayers to be answered and I want the blessing of God in my life. Sometimes people come up to us and ask us why our lives seem so full of adventure and why God somehow always meets our every need. We ask them two questions:

1) Do you tithe? You cannot expect the Lord to bless you financially if you do not honor a biblical principle. We find that many people are able to say yes to this question.

2) The next question we ask is "What have you done for the poor and needy?" It is amazing to see how many people walk away, start giving a list of excuses, or put their heads down when we ask this question.

One of my favorite Scriptures is Isaiah 58:6-12: "Is this not the fast which I choose, to loosen the bonds of wickedness, to undo the bands of the yoke, and to let the oppressed go free, and break every yoke? Is it not to divide your bread with the hungry, and bring the homeless poor into the house; when you see the naked, to cover him; and not to hide yourself from your own flesh? Then your light will break out like the dawn, and your recovery will speedily spring forth; and your righteousness will go before you; the glory of the Lord will be your rear guard. Then you will call, and the Lord will answer; you will cry, and He will say, 'Here I am.' If you remove the yoke from your midst, the pointing of the finger, and speaking wickedness, and if you give yourself to the hungry, and satisfy the desire of the afflicted, then your light will rise in darkness, and your gloom will become like mid-day. And the Lord will continually guide you, and satisfy your desire in scorched places, and give your bones; and you will be like a watered garden, and like a spring of water whose waters do not fail. And those from among you will rebuild the ancient ruins; you will raise up the age-old foundations; and you will be called the repairer of the breach, the restorer of the streets in which to dwell."

As I read this Scripture I find six things that the Lord requires of us and at least ten blessings: We are told:

1) to loose the bonds of wickedness
2) to let the oppressed go free
3) to break every yoke
4) to share our bread with the hungry
5) to bring the homeless poor into our homes
6) to cover the naked

When we do these things, these promises result:

1) your light will break forth like the dawn
2) your healing will spring up speedily
3) righteousness shall go before you
4) you shall call and the Lord shall answer
5) the Lord will guide you continually
6) your desire will be satisfied with good things
7) your bones will be made strong
8) you will be like a watered garden whose waters will not fail
9) your ancient ruins shall be rebuilt
10) you shall raise up the foundations of many generations.

May this Scripture live in all our lives! God's goodness is overwhelming to me and so is His pain as He looks at a wounded generation that has been told that abortion is the answer to their problems, that children are not a blessing, but a curse. May God bless each of us as we move toward bringing the Kingdom of God on earth and as we commit ourselves to saving the born and the unborn.

2

Your Family

Your relationship as a married couple and as a family are very important areas to address as you consider living as an extended family.

Called Together

It is crucial for both husband and wife to be in agreement about this ministry. This is not something that should be done because one or the other of you feel called by the Lord. You both must feel the call.

Very often the woman will be the first to receive the vision/call from the Lord for this particular type of ministry. She becomes aware of the need and her heart is moved by the magnitude of the problem. She asks herself, "What can I do?" and enthusiastically shares her vision with her husband. Often, he will proceed to tell her all the reasons why they should reconsider any ministry that would involve taking strange people into their home. As time goes on he will often have a change of heart and the ministry will begin.

This often seems to be the pattern, and I believe that there are some good reasons why the woman receives the Lord's call to this work first:

1) The wife is the one who will be involved in day-to-day living with the young woman who comes into their home. At first this sounds great, but the daily routine can sometimes wear and tear on a person, especially if personalities do not blend. The Lord needs to embed this dream/vision deep within her so that it is something she knows is from Him.

If she jumps in too quickly, she might well become discouraged and put an additional burden on her husband. The wife is often the planner as far as the running of the household is concerned. She is the nester, the one who builds the environment of the home. If this decision is made impulsively, she will not have time to think through some of the major issues that need to be addressed. But when she carries the dream for a time, she not only plans and mentally decorates the room the young woman will live in, she also considers how she will run the household with another person present as well. The Lord knew what He was doing when He gave us nine months to birth a child. By the time the baby gets here, *we are ready*! This same principle applies when we become an extended family.

2) Normally, the wife is the more feeling person of the two, but the husband is usually the one who thinks more logically. He is able to bring some of the more important issues to the fore and help his wife think them through: issues such as finances, lifestyle changes, etc. When the Lord takes His time before moving in the husband's heart, it allows the wife more time to work through some of these issues. An example of how the Lord works in this situation can be found in the story of Ed and Janet Meeks who were houseparents at Sparrow House in Owings Mill, Maryland. They have four children: Amy, Tim, Katie, and Emily.

In 1977 Ed was employed as a personnel manager and he and Janet were taking pre-adoptive infants into their home through a local public agency. Janet remembers standing in the room where the cribs were and having a vision of what it would be like to work not only with the babies, but with their mothers as well. She stated, "I thought how much I'd like to reach the young girls and teach them infant care and parenting skills."

Two months later the Lord touched their hearts and Ed and Janet entered a relationship with Him, and shortly after that, the agency contacted them about a young pregnant girl who had nowhere to live. Would they take her in? They did.

"She was just like a member of the family," Janet says. "When she moved in I wanted to do everything right. I went to the local bookstore to inquire about books to use when working with pregnant teenagers, and there weren't any. But the woman at the bookstore told me about hearing Anne Pierson speak at an Aglow meeting and suggested she and Jim might be able to help me."

Janet didn't approach us right away, but she made a mental note of our names and went on to work with Theresa, who began to blossom in her new environment, and came to know the Lord. "Then I thought, wouldn't it be neat to take in more than one young woman at a time?" recalls Janet, "and I started talking about it to Ed, to our friends, and to anyone I knew! The whole vision of living in a big house and taking in pregnant young women burned in me, although we were nowhere near that situation."

A year after hearing about us, Janet wrote us a letter and she and Ed visited our home in Pennsylvania. Janet recalls, "We felt a real bonding between our two families, and we kept in touch after we parted that day."

Then Janet heard that two maternity home programs were looking for full-time houseparents. "We investigated both programs, and I just knew that we were meant to be the houseparents at one of those homes. Then Ed went to visit our pastor for guidance about the decision. When he came home, he told me the word he received was that it was not the right time. I was crushed. I cried for two months straight at the death of my dream. I had been hanging onto the verse in Habakkuk 2: "Record the vision and inscribe it on tablets, that the one who reads it may run, for the vision is yet for the appointed time.' I felt that this was our appointed time, and here we were missing it!

"During those years, I remember going before God again and again with my vision, and asking Him what was happening here! We were still taking in one pregnant young woman at a time, but my vision was for several. I begged God for the chance to become a houseparent. Then in August of 1983 our youngest daughter was born two months prematurely and was in intensive care for five weeks.

"The Lord brought us through that, but that next January after things had settled down, I went before the Lord again with my same question, asking for guidance. I was led to a Scripture verse that said this would be the time. The Lord showed me that I had been praying for six years, and the seventh year was to be the year of completion. I shared this with Ed, and we began to pray for confirmation.

"First, we received a call from a friend in Tulsa who heard we were involved in the Right to Life movement. She told us the Lord had given her a vision of a large white house with pregnant teenagers in it. Next, a friend of Ed's wrote him that the Lord had told him to tell Ed that he was to build a Sav-A-Baby type of home.

"Then one day Ed and I picked up a new devotional book we had just seen and turned to the Scripture for the day. It was from First Chronicles 22, a passage that describes David commissioning Solomon to build the Temple. After providing Solomon with gold, silver, bronze, and timber, the Lord told him, 'Moreover, there are many workmen with you, stonecutters and masons of stone and carpenters, and all men who are skillful in every kind of work. Of the gold, the silver and the bronze and

14

the iron, there is no limit. Arise and work, and may the Lord be with you.' This was our final confirmation!"

This time when Ed went to his pastor, the pastor also felt that the timing was right. The Board of Deacons had been looking into this type of ministry, and when Ed presented the vision to them, they offered him the job of business administrator for the church, which would include overseeing the future home.

In 1985 things started coming together, and Sparrow House, a beautiful three-story Currier and Ives home with a wrap-around porch, was opened. "It needed cosmetic work," Janet said, "but God provided the laborers. Over 100 people from our church responded to volunteer.

"Through all this, I've learned that it's important to know that it's not your dream, as I used to think of my vision those seven years. It's God's dream. God has a dream for the earth and He looks for a dreamer to place that dream in their heart. And God will go to no end to fulfill that dream completely. When things started happening, they happened so fast, Ed and I had to get out of the way!"

Time Together

Be sure to make time for each other as a couple. You need to have private times together. One of the things you will notice, especially if you currently have small children, is the loss of privacy. Though your children may go to bed early, the young woman will usually stay up until you go to bed. Because of this change in your lifestyle, you will need to be more creative in the times you do have together.

Jim and I would plan walks together around the property. On a few occasions we had bathroom meetings: one of us sitting on the toilet and one on the edge of the tub. We learned to plan special outings. This ministry will take away the problem of taking time alone for granted. Over the years, we have learned to plan, anticipate, and enjoy each moment we have alone together. This has been very good for our marriage.

Another area for consideration is family outings. Many of the activities you plan as a family will now include the young woman who is staying with you (church activities, meals out, special outings to the amusement park, family movies, or circus, etc.). Many of the young women who lived with us experienced some things for the first time as a result of our outings. Some had never been to the beach before, or had never been sight-seeing in Washington, D.C. Others had never been to an art museum, a ball game, or the zoo. We had one young woman who had never had a Christmas tree. She asked us if she could sleep under it, and we made a bed for her near the tree. What a joy it was to open new horizons for them!

There will also be times when you will feel the need to have time alone with just your family. We found that some friends were not enthusiastic about our ministry and they might on occasion invite us but not include the young woman who was living with us. Sometimes we would turn down such invitations, but at other times we felt impressed to go. At those times, we relied on a special outing with her support person, or our back-up couple might have her over to dinner. Overall, we tried to be creative and sensitive at the same time.

Sensitivity

Husbands and wives need to be more sensitive to each other while they are involved in an extended family ministry.

Wives, be careful that you do not relate all your experiences of the day during the first fifteen minutes after your husband walks in the door. Allow him time to unwind, maybe even have dinner, and then sit and talk about the events of the day, decisions which must be made, etc.

Husbands, your wives may need extra love and assurance while another young woman is living with you. Ninety percent of the time she will probably be fine, but there are those moments when the pressures of having another woman living under the same roof require special love and assurance from you. Remember that women are feeling people and have a need to be understood on that level.

Your Pastor

As With Ed and Janet, it is important for you to talk with your pastor/priest and for him to be in agreement with you in taking this step.

Your pastor/priest's approval is important for several reasons. Because he is your spiritual leader, it is important that he approve of the ministry you plan to get involved in. We suggest that you meet with him concerning your leading in this area even before you fill out an application to be an extended family. He may have some areas of concern that you need to address before making this important decision. He may also have words of affirmation. A pastor/priest's affirmation of ministry is a wonderful way to know that it is truly God's leading.

Another reason for getting the pastor/priest's approval is that he needs to be aware of any ministry that is occurring in his church. He needs to be able to understand and maybe even ask you questions concerning this new ministry that the Lord has given you. Because of your ministry, you may open up ministry for many other families in your church.

We recently heard of a church that had home groups. One couple in a home group took a person in need into their home. Within a year's time, five other couples in that group had people living in their homes.

As your pastor is aware of the ministry you are involved in, it is easier for him to minister to you as needs arise. These are just a few of the reasons why his approval is important.

From the ministry or organization's perspective (i.e. the pregnancy counseling center to which you are applying for approval as an extended family) it is absolutely essential that they know your pastor is behind the ministry you are choosing. The ministry as a whole would be in error if they allowed you to serve when your pastor felt you were not ready. If you are called by God, your pastor/priest will be in agreement.

Family and Friends' Reactions

Whenever we feel called by the Lord into a special area of ministry, we make the mistake of believing that everyone around us is going to be as excited about it as we are. This simply is not the case. Jesus had a miraculous ministry and yet there were many who did not understand Him.

> And as Jesus passed on from there, He saw a man, called Matthew, sitting in the tax office; and He said to him,
> 'Follow me!' And he rose, and followed Him. And it happened that as He was reclining at the table in the house, behold many tax-gatherers and sinners came and were dining with Jesus and His disciples. And when the Pharisees saw this, they said to His disciples, 'Why is your Teacher eating with the tax-gatherers and sinners?' But when He heard this, He said, 'It is not those who are healthy who need a physician but those who are sick. But go and learn what this means: I desire compassion, and not sacrifice, for I did not come to call the righteous, but sinners." (Matt. 9:9-13)

Don't be surprised if family members (yes, parents, sisters, and brothers) do not agree with your decision. You may get statements such as "This could ruin your children's lives," or "These women should be punished, not loved." The questions and responses to your decision to minister in this way are many.

Some will be encouraging and some will not.

Be prepared for this, but do not be discouraged by it. Satan would love to discourage you to the point that you would give up this vital and important work. Allow them to state their reasons. Do not feel that you need to defend your position. Some opposed Christ, and some will oppose you.

Children

Our children are often a concern as we approach this ministry. When God puts a call on your life, and it is confirmed in your hearts as a couple, and through your pastor, He will care for your children as well. Because God gave you your children , and if He placed the call on your life, then your children must need this call in their lives as well.

Bring your children into your plans and make sure they are in agreement. If they do not want "people" in their home, you need to hear their cries. Don't be alarmed or threatened if they ask many questions at first about the arrangements. This does not mean they are going to oppose you, it simply means they have questions. The time to look for their response is after all the questions have been answered.

Age is another thing to be considered. Early and late adolescence is a very difficult time for every teenager and young adult. For this reason we do not recommend that you take young women into your home from the time that your sons are twelve until they are out on their own.

A young woman who has been rejected and hurt by a young man may often feel the need for the love of a male. This may often be projected onto a teen-aged son and it can cause a very difficult time for him, the parents and the young woman.

If you find yourself in this position, but still feel a calling from the Lord in this area, we recommend that you become a back-up couple for the ministry. This means that when a couple who is housing a young woman would need an evening out or a few days away, the young woman would stay at your home. Because the visits are short, there is usually not time for a problem to develop in the area of her relationship to your son. You could even serve as a back-up for several families at once. There is a great need for people who are willing to serve in this capacity, and couples in ministry full-time will attest to the fact that it is a very important ministry indeed!

Often questions come up about small children in the home. These need to be answered on an individual basis. If you feel you are already stretched about as far as you can be stretched, then we do not advise taking in a young woman who may have many needs.

If, on the other hand, you are already involved in some activities outside your home or are feeling the need for more involvement in ministry, young children in the home can be an asset, especially in helping the young woman in a crisis pregnancy make a decision about her own child. To live in a home where there are young children is a great way to see the reality of parenting.

If you do have young children you will need to take this into consideration as you make the rules for your household. You should have a section in your rules regarding the young woman's involvement with your children. State clearly whether she will be allowed to discipline the children or not. Write out what she should do if she sees the children misbehaving. Let her know from the beginning what the arrangements will be as far as babysitting is concerned. These are all important areas which must be addressed. You will find that when you settle these issues before she comes to live with you, you will not have nearly as many problems as you would have if you did not do so. If you wait for incidents to occur, you will find you will be constantly moving from crisis to crisis.

Extended family living is a ministry that can enhance your marriage and your home. We have found that over the years it has increased our sensitivity to each other. We have seen our children become caring and loving people through our example. As Jim and I look back over our twenty-five plus years of marriage, we agree that the most fulfilling and challenging years have been the years we have lived in an extended family. We have raised our children and spent most of our married life in this lifestyle. Would we do it again? Absolutely!

3

Who Is She

In Matthew 25 we have a powerful Scripture concerning how God views our efforts to reach out to those in need of housing and other basic necessities.

> "'For I was hungry, and you gave me something to eat; I was thirsty, and you gave Me drink; I was a stranger, and you invited Me in; naked, and you clothed Me; I was sick, and you visited Me; I was in prison, and you came to Me.' Then the righteous will answer Him saying, 'Lord, when did we see You hungry, and feed You, or thirsty, and give You drink? And when did we see You a stranger, and invite You in, or naked, and clothe You? And when did we see You sick, or in prison, and come to You?' And the King will answer and say to them, 'Truly I say to you, to the extent that you did it to one of these brothers of Mine, even the least of them, you did it to Me.'" (Matt. 25:35-40)

Just as the King rewarded those who helped the hungry and thirsty, naked, sick, or imprisoned, He will also reward those who reach out in Christian love to offer a hand to the homeless and fatherless in their time of greatest need.

There are five areas to consider as we move towards housing young women:

1. Who needs housing?
2. Background
3. Feelings
4. Pressures
5. Potentials

As we look into each of these areas, it is important to remember that no one fits every description. Each is unique in her gifts, her abilities, her past experiences, and her hurts.

Who Needs Housing?

Let's consider this by looking at five young women in crisis pregnancy. Which of these women do you think became an unwed mother? Which ones needed housing?

Melissa is nineteen years old and presently attending a technical school in order to become a veterinary assistant. She is a talented pianist. At present, she is not dating a particular fellow. She comes from a middle-class Catholic family. In her senior year of high school she gave her heart to the Lord, but has drifted away recently. She does not use drugs or alcohol, except for social drinking.

Heida, twenty-two, is a graduate student. She has been dating one young man for the last four years who is also in graduate school. They have been having some problems in their relationship recently, but continue to plan for their future together. Her father died when she was very young and her mother has remarried. There are three children from her mother's first marriage, and three from the second. The second set of children are much younger than her, but Heida has a good relationship with them, as well as with her mother.

Josephine, fifteen, is a sophomore in high school. She comes from a very deprived background. Living in a home with no running water and with two brothers who have active TB, the future does not look promising for her. Her father and mother are alcoholics. In spite of these problems, she has some hope. She is very pretty and well-liked in school, and has no trouble getting good grades.

Pearl, twenty-one, comes from a strict Christian family. There are six brothers and sisters, all very close. After graduating from high school, she went to work with her father. Her favorite pastime is memorizing and reading poetry. She dates from time to time. She recently had an abortion without her parents' knowledge.

Rosemary, sixteen, is in a foster home because she has constantly run away from home. She is athletic, loves a good time, and has missed a lot of school due to truancy. Her parents are dedicated Christians and are very hurt and upset by Rosemary, who is their oldest child.

Which of these young women became an unwed mother? Which ones needed housing? Each one became an unwed mother, and all of them lived with Jim and me.

Crisis pregnancy and other areas of woundedness cross all ethnic, religious, social, and educational backgrounds. There is no group that will not be touched by this problem. We must not be so naive as to think that these women come only from non-Christian homes. Over the years, we have found that one in four of the women who lived with us were from Christian families.

We are frequently asked, "Why would a young woman from a Christian home need housing?" In general, we in the housing movement have made some basic mistakes in drawing up our housing programs and in presenting them to the public. We have given the impression that housing is only for the "down and outer." This should not be the case. The reality is that housing should be seen as a very positive option for any young woman experiencing a major crisis in her life.

When a Christian family seeks housing for their daughter, it will usually be for one of these reasons:

1) there are other siblings or grandparents in the family who need to be sheltered from the circumstances;

2) relatives and/or church members might be applying negative pressure to the situation;

3) the young woman needs to be in a more intense Christian setting to take some of the pressure and tension off her parents, and off herself as well;

4) there is need for additional emotional, physical, and spiritual support during this difficult time;

5) there is a need to get away from a boyfriend;

6) the young woman needs to continue her schooling, and is unable to do so in her present situation.   Our philosophy has always been that we need to keep the Body of Christ strong, and one way to do this is to be available to meet a need in the body. As these people are helped and encouraged during a difficult time in their lives, they will hopefully reach out later to help and encourage others. There are young women who have lived with us who are now serving in Christian ministries all over the country.

Anne, Ray, and Julie are examples of Christians whom we helped who are now reaching out to help others. Anne and her husband Ray were first exposed to the pro-life movement when their daughter Julie became pregnant in 1977. Their Florida pastor was originally from Pennsylvania and directed them to Jim and me at the House of His Creation. Julie came to live with us in January of 1978 and when her baby was born, Anne flew up to visit.

As Anne puts it: "I remember the House of His Creation as a place of both joy and tears. I was so touched, that when I came home to the family, I knew that God had placed a call on my life to do the same thing in this area. I couldn't understand why no one else felt the same way I did!"

Ray was open to helping, but he did not feel they were to open their home. "So I had to let my vision die," said Anne, "which I did for five years."

Then, a group at Anne's church started getting together to discuss what they could do to help unwed mothers in their area. After much prayer, someone from the group suggested starting a home like the House of His Creation.

When her church group decided to start a home, Anne knew that the vision she had let die was finally about to become a reality in God's timing. She contacted Jim and me, now at Loving and Caring, and in 1986 His Caring Place was opened in Pompano Beach. The home is truly a family ministry, with Ray and Julie serving enthusiastically on the Board of Directors, and Anne serving as its President.

We need to move towards offering housing as just one of many available options; not as a last resort. There is no question that young women who are housed in individual Christian homes or in Christian group homes usually will make more life changes than young women who come to a center for counseling one hour a week. To be able to see the Christian life lived out in a family is one of the greatest witnesses of Christ we can give them.

The reason housing has not been a more viable option is threefold:

1) Organizations and ministries have a mind set that only young women who have nowhere else to go should be housed;
2) housing programs take a great deal of coordination, often by volunteers;

27

3) last, and most important, there are simply not enough couples willing to open their homes to extended family living.

Background

Let's look at some background information that will help us learn more about young women in crisis and how we can relate to them.

In our society today, it is estimated that one out of every two marriages end in divorce. This means that approximately forty percent to fifty percent of our young people have lived in single-parent families at one time or another during their childhood. This has a major impact on their ability to handle the pressures of life.

Fathers

The husband's role in this ministry is as important and vital as the wife's. He provides, maybe for the first time, a positive Christian male image. Many people have never known any man who was faithful to a woman, much less one who lived a Christian life. What a wonderful opportunity to change someone's entire concept of "manliness" and what it can mean.

A large majority of young people, and especially women in crisis pregnancy, come from homes with poor father images. On one hand, the father may be entirely absent from the home through death, desertion, or divorce. Or, he may be in the home but nonetheless present a poor father image to his children: he could be an alcoholic, workaholic, or even "church-aholic." He and his wife may be having marital problems. He may be abusive to his children (including incidents of incest). Nine out of ten of the young women who lived with us came from families with poor father images.

We have noticed that when a good father image is missing, young women display certain traits more prominently than do young women who have positive father images. Some of these traits are:

1) Inadequate skills relating to males in general. These young women generally did not relate well to Jim and would have their primary relationship with me, attempting to do all the communicating through me.

2) Inability to choose good dating partners. We found that many of the young women who lived with us did one of two things: they either dated someone older than themselves (i.e. a fifteen-year-old girl dating a twenty-three-year-old guy) or they dated men with numerous problems of their own. In many cases, both needed individual help and yet they clung to each other, refusing to be separated.

3) Many of the young women with poor father images had difficulty relating to the other young women in our home. They were often distant or had behavior that turned the other young women off. We found that as their relationships with Jim improved, very often their relationships with their peers also improved.

4) In spite of the fact that their mothers had had negative experiences with men, they subconsciously seemed to feel that not to have a man was an even greater disaster. To not have a man was worse than having one who mistreated you or with whom you could not get along.

Why is this? Women have a basic need for a male covering— a father. If this is taken away from us, or is defective in any way, a young woman will seek to replace it through another male, usually a boyfriend.

A poor father image can also affect our spiritual life. In many cases, we relate to God in the same way we relate to our earthly fathers. It becomes difficult for us to see God as a loving Father when our earthly father has failed us. Another problem is that often the weakness which has been evident in our earthly father becomes a weakness we transfer to our image of God our

Father. If our father is undependable and/or suffers from alcoholism, it is hard to trust a dependable God. If our father is a hard disciplinarian, then we see God as hard to please. He will "get you" if you do something wrong. If our father's love is conditional, we see God's love as conditional.

As the young woman living with you begins to open up, take careful note of her relationship to her father. This knowledge can be very helpful in showing you how to pray for her. It can also give you a better understanding of how she sees God the Father. As you understand this, you will be better able to present God to her in the areas where she needs the most healing.

When we house a young woman whose father is an alcoholic, we want to show her that God is steadfast: the same yesterday, today, and forever. Alcoholic fathers may be great dads when they are sober, but a family never knows when they will come home drunk or when their moods will change as a result of drinking. This can lead their children to see God as untrustworthy. By showing them God's steadfastness, we produce healing in them. Never assume that everyone sees God the same way you do. Each of us has our own strengths and weaknesses in this area.

Think about your own father and your relationship with him. You may not have had a poor father image at all, but no one is perfect. Where was your father weak? Ask God to show you the weaknesses in your dad; then ask yourself if you have allowed these weaknesses to interfere with your relationship to God. Pray and ask God to reveal any areas that need healing. Many people who seek God regarding this have received healing and have found a fresh newness in their relationship to Him.

One of the things I love about the Lord is that as we give ourselves to others and seek His will and healing for their lives, we are often healed ourselves.

We've spent a lot of time on fathers, because this is an important area in your home, as well as in group homes. The young women who live with you will grow as a result being around a positive father image. Often, ideas and wounds from the past are completely healed simply by observing a positive father. Other areas of healing occur as a relationship is nurtured between the young woman and the couple she is living with.

Psalms 34:17-18 gives us a Scripture of promise:
> When the righteous cry for help, the Lord hears, and delivers them out of all their troubles. The Lord is near to the broken-hearted, and saves the crushed in Spirit.

Mothers

Now let's talk about the mother's role. The wife, of course, will function in the daily role of house management and principal communicator. Mothers are the communicators in the home. They are often the "person in the middle" in the family structure. Because they are generally feeling-oriented, they are more in tune with how the family is feeling. Because of this, mothers have a tendency sometimes to be too protective because they are worried about their child's feeling level.

Mothers are extremely important to their children. A child feels it is more acceptable for the father to leave the home than for the mother. When the mother leaves the children, they have a sense of worthlessness. "If my mother doesn't want me, who could possibly want me?"

If the mother of the young woman living with you is displaying bitterness, remember that she was not born bitter. It has been built in her through years of discouragement and pain. When you see a mother who is bitter towards her children, it usually is because she has been pushed beyond her limits. Mothers don't become bitter overnight, but only after years of trying and failing with their children, their husbands, possibly their own mothers, and other important people in their lives.

31

Some mothers are so good at communicating with their children that they totally take over this role, leaving their husband with very few ways to relate to his children, especially as they grow older. I can't tell you how many interviews we have had where the mother has done all the talking and the father has sat there saying nothing. There have been times when I have even asked the father a direct question and the mother has answered for him.

The role of the mother is important. Your relationship as a mother figure will do much to help the young woman in your home. Through you, she will mature, become responsible, build her self-esteem, learn what a woman of God is, and feel God's love.

Jim and I learned very early in our marriage that it was important to have definite ways for our children to communicate with Jim. I am definitely the communicator in our family, and Jim is more quiet. We realized that this could become a problem for us, especially as our children got older. For this reason we made a rule that I would never give permissions. Even today, our children know to go to their dad if they want to get something, go somewhere, or need any type of permission. We thank the Lord for revealing this to us as we reached out to others. There is no question that the more you respond to the hurting and wounded in this world, the more you learn about your own family structure.

Behavior Problems

Because of our varied backgrounds, personality conflicts may arise between the couple and the young woman living with them. Issues will surface that you won't understand or know how to handle. When this occurs, ask the Lord to love her through you, especially in those times when you are finding it hard to love her yourself. God brings people into our lives to teach us. Take this opportunity to ask Him in prayer why a particular behavior problem is showing itself before you jump on her about it. God will furnish insight into her behavior.

We had this happen when a young woman came to live with us and immediately started hoarding food—taking food out of the kitchen up to her room. Jim and I were puzzled, as there was always plenty to eat in our home, and it was readily available.

In prayer one day, the Lord reminded us that this young woman had come from a very deprived background. He showed us that she hoards because she thinks she is going to be hungry again. (This same girl, when offered clothes from your pregnancy center or boutique, may frequently take more than she can possibly wear.)

To handle the hoarding, we found the best remedy was reassurance. We began to reassure her daily about the fact that we will have enough food to eat. As I unloaded the groceries I would say, "If we run out of fruit, we can get some more," or "If we run out of fruit, we could make cookies or pop some popcorn. That would be fun, wouldn't it?"

At mealtime, Jim might say, "After dinner tonight we can pop some popcorn or have a snack." We constantly reinforced the fact that more food was coming. We found that in a few weeks her behavior changed. If this had not worked, then and only then would we sit down and talk with her about her behavior.

> I will instruct you and teach you in the way you would go. I will counsel you with my eye upon you. (Ps. 32:8)

No matter what her background or the differences between you, the Lord will guide and direct you in handling whatever may arise.

Feelings

Feelings affect all of us all of the time. There are good and bad feelings. In a later chapter, we will discuss all the feelings that

33

take place during the settling-in process. There is no question that during this time there are a mixture of feelings for everyone involved. As we consider the young woman staying with you, let's look at some areas where feelings need to be understood and worked through.

She is coming to live with you. She wants to be loved and accepted, even though she may not understand what love is. She needs to be loved, but it may be that when you say "love," it means "physical love" to her. Your example of love in your family will help her understand love better.

As Christians, we have a much greater understanding of what real love is. The more we experience Christ, the more we understand sacrificial love. But if you have only lived in the secular world and have only experienced love from the secular world, then love to you is mostly physical.

As we talk about feelings, another important factor you will learn to understand is that her own crisis may be so great that she can't think of anything else. In the case of a woman in crisis pregnancy, this can include the baby's life or its needs. This affects her decision-making ability, especially in the area of self-care. Help her accept and deal with her feelings and gently bring other areas such as the baby into focus for her.

You may be a childbirth instructor or have been through childbirth yourself. You know that she really needs to be walking every day, exercising, eating the right foods, and doing all those things that are so important to pregnant women. In spite of all your knowledge, she is sitting there with her potato chips and Coke in front of the television set and saying, "I don't need to walk. My mother had an hour labor and I will too." This can be really frustrating for those "moms" who are into nutrition or are physically motivated.

There will be some young women who will be very motivated physically. One young woman we had was studying to be a professional dancer. She watched her diet and danced through

34

her whole pregnancy because she didn't want to lose that ability. She made tremendous sacrifices to give her baby life. She had to leave her dancing career behind for a year. You have a few of these highly motivated women, but they are not the norm! Most of them are not motivated, and it's hard to motivate them.

I suggest you don't get too hung up on her eating or exercise habits. Later we will discuss some possible rules revolving around eating habits, but there are many creative ways around this without creating a scene.

1) Don't keep junk food in the house. Make sure you have good nutritious snacks on hand at all times. Set a good example yourself, even though this might involve sacrifices for your family.

2) Give her opportunities to plan meals with your guidance.

3) Walk with her. It won't hurt you to walk a mile a day, and the time can be used for conversation and sharing together. Years have gone by, but some of the young women we've lived with still remember the conversations we had on our walks. I'm a great story-teller, and as I'd walk along I'd tell them the story of a particular little flower and build it into a great spiritual lesson about the flower that bloomed because it was glad God made it and put it there, even though it appeared nobody was ever going to pay any attention to it. My moral was: do the best you can, not because of the applause you will receive, but because you simply want to do your best. Today girls will say, "Do you remember the flower story? I've never forgotten the flower story."

4) Be an encourager. Look for every opportunity to praise her. Keep in mind the advice Paul gives us in 1 Thess. 5:11:

"Therefore, encourage one another and build one another up, just as you are doing."

Pressures

Parent, peer, and boyfriend pressures must be taken into

consideration. Parents may be pushing her in one direction or another, even giving ultimatums. Boyfriends can be very opinionated. All of these pressures will affect her. (We had many young women who felt that their boyfriends were all they had and they must listen to them at all costs!)She may feel rebellious toward her parents and unwilling to listen to any advice they give. She may be struggling between boyfriend and parents, both with different opinions.

The opinions of ministers, her teachers, etc. also take their toll. Depending upon how she feels about them as individuals, she will take or leave their guidance.

One young woman I talked to had talked to four pastors before coming to see me, and all four had told her to get an abortion. She was bound and determined not to get an abortion and kept looking for a Christian who would tell her something else. I was the first Christian she met who presented another option to her. We think that doesn't happen today, but it does.

Doctors and other medical personnel are also capable of applying pressure. I once had a young woman who was hospitalized to control a diabetic condition. A doctor from the prenatal clinic walked into her room and told her that if she didn't get an abortion she was going to die. It was a lie, but as a layperson, how was my opinion going to compete with a doctor's? I offered to take her to another physician for a second opinion, but she refused. The doctor had scared her and she wasn't willing to take the chance that she would die, so we lost the baby. That's the kind of pressure a professional can apply. We have to love and encourage, not condemn her for giving in to pressure, because in some situations it can really be intense.

For women who are in a crisis pregnancy, or sexually active, our society (TV, magazines, books, music) has been selling her "sex, sex, sex." Sex has become a commodity. After a date, teens ask each other, "Coke, pizza, or sex?" The sexual experience that was supposed to be special and beautiful has more often than not left her pregnant and alone. Why didn't it work out for her the way it does in the movies? Why is she the one who got pregnant rather than her friends?

Previous behavior can put additional pressure on her relationship with you. Maybe in the past she had a problem with authority, decision-making, seeing things through to an end, etc. Now she is faced with a situation which requires all of these qualities, and she has never handled any of them well.

When Mary Lou came to live with us it didn't take long to discover that she had never had any responsibility in her home. When her parents told her to make her bed, or gave her some household assignments, and she did not do them, they simply did them for her. If she left for school with her bed unmade, it would be made by the time she returned. Mother might bawl her out when she got home, but she rarely had to make her bed, and she had learned to turn off the verbal reprimands. The end result of this type of parenting was a pregnant daughter who thought the world would take care of her. She really believed that if she waited long enough, someone would do the job for her. You can well imagine that this simply is not true in the job world, nor would her husband in later years appreciate this kind of attitude.

Jim and I realized very quickly that we had a challenge on our hands. The first item of business was to give her basic household chores, including bed-making, each day. If the jobs were not done, she would lose privileges until they were done. Sometimes she would go to bed without television rather than give in to the chores. But they would be waiting for her in the morning. We solved the bed-making problem by making a rule that if her bed was not made by 10:00 AM, it would be stripped from the bottom and rolled up in a big ball on her bed. Once she tried to go to bed without making her bed, and I waited until she had gone to sleep, then woke her up and had her make it. After getting her up one time, the bed was made every day. I used this technique on other women who lived with us and it always worked!

After she had been with us for about a month, her parents invited her home for the weekend. That particular day she had the assignment of ironing the curtains that had been washed the day before. She put the ironing off all day, hoping that her father would come to pick her up and she could leave the ironing undone. I knew what she was doing and waited patiently. I talked with Jim and together we agreed that she would not be allowed to leave unless the curtains were done.

Sure enough, her father arrived about three in the afternoon and the curtains were still in the clothes basket. She ran to get her suitcase as I greeted her father. I told her father that we had a small problem which needed to be taken care of. I explained the situation to him and told him that he could either wait for her or, if he didn't have time to wait, we could postpone the visit. He agreed to wait.

Mary Lou came into the living room with her suitcase and I told her that before she could leave she needed to finish the curtains. By this time her father had taken a seat on the sofa and began to read a magazine. She looked at her dad to help her, but he kept reading. She then stomped out and quickly ran an iron over the curtains. She came back and began to pick up her suitcase. I asked her to wait just a minute until I checked the curtains. When I checked, they were barely ironed and so I called her and told her they would have to be done again. By this time she was **angry**. She did the curtains and before she left, her father thanked me for my courage. He said he wished that he could be that firm with her.

I wasn't sure she would ever come back, but on Sunday evening she returned. From that time on things begin to improve. By the time she left our home shortly after the birth of her child, she was like a different person. When her dad came to take her home for good, she came running down the stairs, suitcase in hand, and a smile on her face. "Dad, you are going to be so proud of me at home now. I make my bed. I can clean the house. Why, I even eat peas!"

Sometimes it involves taking a risk that a young woman may never return in order to teach some important lesson needed for her life. But there needs to be firmness applied with love. It is wrong to simply be firm without establishing a love relationship. This does not mean that for the first few weeks you let her walk all over you. It does mean that you make your expectations clear, stand firm as far as her responsibility is concerned, and then encourage her whenever you can.

As you deal with the pressures in your life and in hers, remember to stay in a neutral position, showing her facts, but never putting down the people in her life. She may say she thinks her mother is a terrible person, but you must never agree with her. Instead, try to help her see that when people are hurting themselves, they sometimes say and do things that don't seem fair, or may not be fair. Ask her if she has ever done something she wishes she could take back. Help her work through forgiveness for her parents and all those who have hurt her. Pray for her parents, and if you recognize that you have anger and resentment towards them yourself, ask God's forgiveness.

Another area of pressure for the woman in crisis pregnancy is the decision about the baby. This is probably one of the biggest decisions of her life, and yet she may never before have been allowed to make even the most insignificant decision. You may have to give her basic lessons in decision-making. Why not start by giving her a voice in the menu planning? "What should we have for dinner/dessert?" Let her place the furniture in her own room. These little decisions will help you build your relationship with her and help her increase her decision-making ability and her self-esteem.

Potentials

She needs to be able to depend on someone. Some questions which might be going through her mind are: "Can I trust them?"

"Do they really care about me?" If she finds she can trust you, be prepared to see changes you never dreamed possible.

An important thing to remember is that she comes to you with a value system already in place. Her value system may be totally different from yours, but it is a value system nonetheless. Build from her point of view. Initially, find something you can agree on and discuss that. Maybe the only thing you can agree on at first is the need for a clean home, or your mutual love for children. Find a place to start and honor her values in that area. Don't tear down everything she believes, even when you feel she is totally wrong. Give God time to work inside her heart. Your life example will speak more for the validity of your values than all your words.

Your young woman once had dreams and hopes of what she would like her life to say. It might seem that all her life goals are lost forever because of her crisis. You can help her set her goals and rebuild her dreams. We all need goals in our lives.

In all these areas, remember she is a child of God, created in His image, unique and special, deserving of your care.

Be prepared to learn, grow, cry, laugh, meet new friends, hurt, love, and know Jesus better than ever before. We can change the world for Jesus, for the women we love, and for their unborn children.

4

Self-Esteem

Self-esteem is important to each of our lives. It is something we all must deal with. It begins its development in our childhood. God created us to be loved, cared for, and to have a sense of His purpose and love for us. But because we are imperfect, our self-esteem sometimes gets damaged.

What is self-esteem? Webster's dictionary defines it as "a confidence and satisfaction in oneself: self-respect."

Let's look at one of the most important Scriptures related to self-esteem:

> 'Teacher, which is the greatest commandment in the Law?' And He said to him, 'You shall love the Lord your God with all your heart, and with all your soul, and with all your mind.' This is the great and foremost commandment. The second is like it, You shall love your neighbor as yourself.' (Matt. 22:36-39)

In order to fulfill the second commandment, to "love your neighbor as yourself," it is important to fulfill the first. How do we love the Lord our God with all our hearts, souls, and minds?

Our hearts are the feeling level of our beings. We all have felt the need for something more. It is because of that feeling and the search to find it that we become God's children. We realize our sin, repent, and find new life in Him. From that point on, we are new creatures.

Once we have become new creatures through a change of heart, we develop our souls and minds.

Our souls are developed through spending time with the Lord. Being in the Word, having a quiet time, and fellowshipping with other believers all serve to develop and nurture our souls.

Unfortunately, we often do not make this a priority in our lives. But the Lord put these three parts of us (heart, soul, and mind) in a special order and they need to remain in that order. If we try to develop our minds without getting our relationship with the Lord (hearts) in order, and without developing our souls relationship with Him, our minds, the vital link to self-esteem, will not develop as they should.

The third part of this important triangle, our minds, is addressed in Romans 12:2:

> And do not be conformed to this world, but be
> transformed by the renewing of your mind, that
> you may prove what the will of God is, that
> which is good and acceptable and perfect.

Our daily walk, our actions, and the words we speak reflect the condition of our minds. Our minds direct our outward actions. When our hearts, souls, and minds are in good health, high self-esteem is automatic. At this point we are ready to "Love our neighbor as ourselves."

The young women who come to live with us are our neighbors. We need to look a little deeper into the self-esteem issue from their perspective. Matthew 22:36-39 is our foundation. Now we are ready to consider some other issues in this great battle for a positive self-esteem.

SELF-ESTEEM

"You shall love the Lord your God with all your heart, and with all your soul, and with all your mind" (Matt. 22:37).

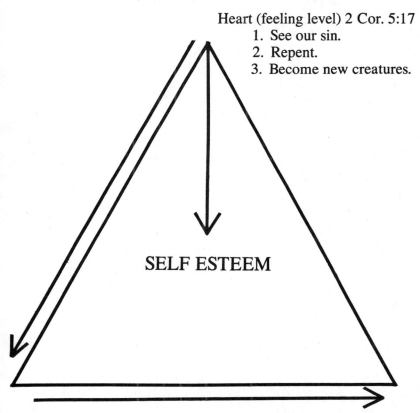

Heart (feeling level) 2 Cor. 5:17
1. See our sin.
2. Repent.
3. Become new creatures.

SELF ESTEEM

Soul (inner strength)
1. Quiet time.
2. Time in the Lord.
3. Fellowship with other believers.

Mind (outer actions)
1. Right attitudes.
2. How we handle things externally.
3. Our words.

So many young people feel inferior—they feel that they are not as good as others, not as pretty, do not have as much ability, are not as smart, etc. There is nothing that is more important to our emotional well-being than to love ourselves, and the only way we can love ourselves is to know how Christ loves us. When that occurs, we begin to have a love relationship with ourselves and all kind of healing occurs within us.

James Dobson, in "Preparing for Adolescence," says: "We all have human worth, yet so many young people conclude that they're somehow different—that they're truly inferior—that they lack the necessary ingredients for dignity and worth."[1]

There are three levels of low self-esteem. Let's look at them:

Level One: Everyone's self-esteem is lowered from time to time when some event, activity, embarrassing situation, etc. occurs. Overall, we may feel good about ourselves and about life, but occasionally something embarrassing happens and we fall into this level-one category. The more we realize our value in the eyes of God, the better we are able to bounce back from each disappointing or embarrassing situation.

One example of this level is a situation that happened to me when I was in seventh grade. For some unknown reason my skirt came unzipped, and as I stepped off the school bus at the end of the day it fell down around my ankles. The other children on the bus laughed and all I remember is dropping my books, grabbing my skirt, and heading for home as quickly as possible. Upon my arrival, I told my mother the awful thing that had happened to me and assured her that I could never ride the school bus again.

She listened to my story and agreed that it must have been very embarrassing for me. After she had allowed me to get over the initial trauma, she let me know that I would have to ride the bus the next day. I insisted I couldn't, and she told me I had to. I was convinced that she had no feeling for my situation. How would I ever face the gang again?

The next morning I waited as long as I could and then began my trip to the bus. Sure enough the other children were still laughing and that day was a difficult one for me. But in less than a week it was old news and someone else had done something else embarrassing. It was easy to laugh at them, but it certainly was not easy to be laughed at!

Let me give you another example which happened to us as an extended family. A young woman named Sally was living with us. One of the things we try to do is to find ways to incorporate a young woman's life into ours and at the same time to heal her relationship with her parents. One of our methods involves having our guest become involved in our menu planning.

I often ask a young woman if she has a favorite recipe. She may remember something she loved that her mother made. Then I suggest that she call and get the recipe. If there is any kind of communication between mother and daughter, this type of call will help heal the relationship. The mother senses appreciation from her child because she wants to cook one of the dishes she makes. The daughter has a way to talk with her mother without the usual communication problems because they are sharing something they can agree on. If there have been severe communication problems between mother and daughter, I usually advise the young woman to simply get the recipe and thank her mother. I urge her not to let the conversation move into other areas that could cause the phone call to become a disaster.

Sally followed our advice and got her mother's chili recipe. The phone conversation went well and Sally was very excited about the possibility of cooking her favorite recipe for us. She made it pretty clear that she wanted to do this all by herself. So we got the ingredients she needed and we gave her the kitchen as her private domain for the afternoon.

As we sat down at the table, Jim blessed the meal and immediately put a spoonful of chili in his mouth. I looked at him and knew something was wrong. I very carefully tasted the chili. It was terrible! There was no way we could eat it.

I asked Sally to tell me about her chili. It was crucial to save her from as much embarrassment as possible. If we had said, "What's wrong with this chili?" we would have only made the matter worse. By this time she had tasted it, as had our children. (Thank goodness we had taught our children that they are never to criticize other people's cooking! They may say they do not care for something, but they are never allowed to make fun or to make a comment such as "I don't like that," or "This is terrible.")

Sally began to unravel the story for us. She admitted that she had left the chili and it had burned. She thought she had remembered her mother telling her that whenever something was burned, putting peanut butter in it would remove the burnt taste. "I put a whole jar of peanut butter in it, hoping that you wouldn't notice it was burned," she told us.

As usual, Jim saved the day. "Well, you know, I think that principle is right," he said. "You would never know that this chili was burned! Let's clear the table and I will treat the family to dinner at McDonald's." The important thing at this moment was to save her dignity. Whenever a level-one incident happens to us or some other member of our families, we must be aware of the importance of preserving their dignity.

Level Two: Young people with level-two low self-esteem have a particular area in their lives that will not go away. It may be something about their appearance, their scholastic ability, athletic performance, a lack of money, etc. It is important to remember that eighty percent of the teenagers in our society do not like the way they look.[2] Generally, these young people do well in other areas, but this particular area nags at them constantly. Most of us have experienced a level-two difficulty as teenagers and young adults but we overcome it as we mature.

One of the things that contributes to a level-two self-esteem is the teasing and embarrassment that a young person may receive from their peers or a close family member as a child. As we raise our children, we need to ask God to make us sensitive in these areas.

Level Three: Teens or young adults at this level hurt most of the time. Generally, young people who fall into this category have the other two levels affecting them, as well as family problems (divorce, alcoholism, abuse, etc.) a handicap (physical, learning disability, etc.) or some other extenuating circumstance (extreme shyness, loss of a loved one, personal sickness, pregnancy). Many of the young women who will live with you will fall into a level-three low self-esteem. God may bring these people to you to bring healing into their lives.

Level one is usually overcome in a short period of time. Level two is usually overcome by maturity. Level three can be overcome only with the love and healing power of Christ.

According to Milton Strommen in *The Five Cries of Youth*, young people are so much more vulnerable to low self-esteem because they are caught in an age between childhood and adulthood in a society which is terrified by them. For most young people, the ages between thirteen and twenty-five mark a period when they have none of the privileges of childhood, nor the freedoms of adulthood.

It is important to remember that we should not judge a young person by his chronological age. A twenty-five-year-old can be functioning at a twelve-year-old maturity level, while a fifteen-year-old may have matured beyond her age.

When low self-esteem occurs, the young person feels worthless, lonely, and is generally very critical about himself/herself. These teens may come across as super-cool, extremely shy, unwilling to attempt anything, or anywhere in between!

Now let's consider some particular areas that are affected by low self-esteem. An interesting point Strommen brings out is that the youth most troubled by self-criticism (low self-esteem) are as likely as others to affirm that they are forgiven by God. They intellectually acknowledge God's forgiveness, but emotionally they do not live in an awareness of God's acceptance. They remain preoccupied with standards and the task of "making it" in the eyes of others.[3] Therefore, when a crisis such as pregnancy comes into their lives, they experience tremendous self-condemnation.

Romans 8:1 tells us:
"There is therefore now no condemnation for those who are in Christ Jesus."

If someone who lives with you comes across as super-cool, she is probably afraid of rejection and very scared inside. Don't let her exterior fool you. She needs to be esteemed and needs to hear encouragement from you.

Young people lacking self-confidence will often screen out activities in which they might fail, such as crafts, cooking, card games, athletics, etc. It is good to include some of these in your family life (see Chapter 6: Special Occasions and Crafts). I have also found that taking a young woman to get her hair done, or her colors analyzed (usually by a volunteer from our church), to a make-up demonstration, etc., does a great deal to improve her self-esteem.

How Do We Help?

The first question we need to ask ourselves is what is our value system? Do we value people more according to their professions? Do we find ourselves wanting our children to have certain professions? Maybe, deep down inside, we want our child to have the desire to achieve a dream we never realized. When we face these questions squarely and acknowledge our own prejudices, we usually find it improves the way we look at

47

others. Looking at the young woman as a valuable individual regardless of her social status will help raise her self-esteem.

Friendship is another area which improves self-esteem. It takes time to build a relationship, but when a young woman believes you really care about her, this improves her own self-esteem. It gives her value.

Strommen tells us, "Friends are to these people what bread is to the hungry and clothes are to the naked."[4]This is why girls hang onto guys, even when they know it is wrong. What is needed today is a ministry of friendship. Three out of four young people want to be part of a caring, accepting group. Two out of three want a group that, in addition to offering acceptance, also confronts one another with an honest, frank sharing of personal feelings. They want small group experiences that get at the feeling level and help them to come out from under their public posture.[5]

Ross Campbell, in *How to Really Love Your Teenager*, compares the sum total of a young person's emotional needs to an "emotional tank." How these needs are met, through love, understanding, discipline, etc., determines how that person feels (i.e. depressed, angry, content, joyful). How that person's needs are met also determines that person's behavior (obedient, whiny, alert, playful, withdrawn). The fuller the tank, the better the feelings and the behavior. People can be expected to do their best only when their emotional tanks are full.

A climate of warmth encourages self-esteem in several ways. It frees a person to verbalize her feelings and to put into words the emotions that are churning inside. Don't analyze anyone through a problem approach. The issue is not "What is John's problem?" but "What sort of person is John?" Our task is to collaborate with a young person in discovering ways to help him solve his own problems.[6]

All of these things, when covered with prayer and love, will move the young women in your care to improved self-esteem.

They will become more aware of God's love for them. As this happens, they too, will develop a heart, soul, and mind relationship with God, and many will then move into "Loving their neighbors as themselves."

footnotes for chapter 4, Mending Hearts, Mending Lives

[1] James Dobson, *Preparing for Adolescence*, p. 17
[2] Ibid, p. 21
[3] *Milton Strommen*, Five Cries of Youth, p. 16
[4] Ibid, p. 27
[5] Ibid, p. 27
[6] Strommen, *Five Cries of Youth*, p. 3

5

Settling In

The decision has been made, and she is on her way to your home. What is she thinking? Let's look at some of the feelings the young woman might have at this time:

anxiety	fear	frustration	hostility
sadness	anger	joy	loneliness
hope	panic	excitement	grief

What are some of your feelings as her time of arrival approaches? If you think about them carefully, you will see that you are experiencing a mixture of the same feelings. It is important for you to see that you and she have many of the same emotions.

Settling-in is a difficult process for all of us. There are several times in a lifetime when we must settle into a new place or a new set of circumstances. When we marry, go away to school, move or change jobs, or change life situations, a "settling-in" process occurs.

We need to be sensitive to how difficult this process can be. It is definitely harder for the young women coming than it is for us.

You are in familiar surroundings and only one major area of your life is changing. Almost all areas of her life are in turmoil. There is the need to learn the "turf," to meet new people, to understand her surroundings.

I remember when I got a job at the Library of Congress. I was eighteen and in my first year of college and this was my first office job. Being a native of Washington, D.C., I had visited the library before and had seen all the places tourists see, but had never been to the "offices" in the library. In spite of my previous visits, I felt like a total stranger on that first day.

I had so many questions and concerns that there were some things I decided not to ask. One of these was, "Where is the ladies' room?" The result of failing to ask this important question left me running up several floors to the bathroom I used as a tourist. I was exhausted by the end of the day. Thank goodness by the second day I got up enough courage to ask where the bathroom was!

This might sound like an extreme case and you might even ask, "What does this have to do with housing?" I share this part of my life to make you aware of how difficult settling-in can be in any situation. Whether it is a new job or a new home makes little difference. The challenges are basically the same. You are already there and know the routine and what is expected; she is the newcomer and knows nothing except that she needs the job or the place to live. She hopes everyone will like her, and she wants to fit into the routine, drawing as little attention to herself as possible.

Keeping this in mind, there are some practical ways you can help your young woman settle into your home.

1. Be sure that the rules of your household are in writing and have been gone over (see Chapter 10). Hopefully this will happen before she comes to live with you. It is always best to have met her first and for her to have been allowed to visit your

home. This is the perfect time and place to go over your household rules. I recommend that you make a copy for her to keep.

When she arrives at your home to stay, ask if she has any questions about the rules. Make sure that she has a copy of them. (Have an extra copy available just in case.)The rules let the boundaries of our lives be clearly seen. You may be challenged later on some items, but to begin with she will be grateful that at least for now she knows what to expect from you, and what you expect from her.

2. Find out what her favorite foods are and incorporate them into your menu, especially for the first few meals. An excellent way to do this is to have her fill out the form "What I Like To Do." (See Appendix). Your counselor should have had her fill out this form before settling-in occurs. She should make sure you have the form in time to shop for the needed items. This form allows the young woman to list her favorite foods, magazines, crafts, sports, etc.

3. Be sure that on that first day you let her know your wake-up time and bedtimes. It is good to have these in your written rules, but I still always try to remember to say something about this before going to bed the first night.

4. If there are special bathroom rules, make sure you make these clear from the start. If you are a one-bathroom family, there generally needs to be some understanding as to who needs the bathroom when. If dad needs to be at work by 8:00 AM, this needs to be taken into consideration. Work and school schedules should get top priority when scheduling is done because these are set times and must be honored on a daily basis.

If there are special things she needs to know about your bathroom, make sure you explain them on that first day. For instance, you may have a faucet that leaks and needs to be shut tightly. Your toilet handle may need to be jiggled to get it to stop running. Don't assume that she will figure these things out for

53

herself. These are the types of things that build up frustration, cause embarrassment, and generally prolong the settling-in time.

5. Give clear direction concerning apparel around the home. Let her know what you wear around your home in the evenings and in the mornings. Do you lounge around in your nighties at night or are you a family that stays in street clothes until bedtime? Let her know what the attire should be in the morning as well. Do you all come to breakfast in your nighties or is everyone dressed for breakfast? If you are a nightie family in the morning or in the evenings, make sure she has a robe. A surprise in this area can cause great embarrassment which can affect her self-esteem and delay her settling-in process by weeks.

6. Be sure she knows the kitchen and meal routines. Do you eat every meal as a family or are some meals prepared by each person individually? If she is allowed to get food from the kitchen, make sure you explain the layout of the kitchen and the rules for having food in the living room, bedrooms, etc.

All of these items may seem small in nature, but they will help the settling-in process tremendously. Remember you have had years to understand and set the routine for your home. She is a newcomer. Never assume that every household does things the same way you do. Her parents' lifestyle may have been very different from yours. God will bless and guide each of you as you move through this difficult, but fulfilling process of settling-in. All great friendships and love relationships take time and understanding.

6

Building Family

Now that the commitment has been made and living in an extended family is a part of your life, there are some basic things that need to be considered.

Changes

Let's begin by looking at your lifestyle. Whenever there is a change in our lifestyle, adjustments must be made. Remember when you got married? That took some adjustment. Many of you who were two are now three, four, five, or even six. With each new addition to your family new adjustments were required.

Moving into extended family living is simply another adjustment. Be careful that you are not so busy in other areas of your life that you do not have room in your schedule for this new life God has given you. The young woman in your home needs to be your primary ministry. This does not mean you cannot be involved in other things, but it is important for you to recognize her position in relationship to your ministry goals.

Working Situations

In looking at working situations, I would like to address two particular areas: the working mother, and the husband who is away a great deal with his job.

If both of you work full-time, the young woman who lives with you needs to be carefully screened. For instance, if you have a young woman who is in college most of the day or has a job of her own, your work schedule may not be a problem. If the young woman would be staying alone at home all day, I would not recommend her for your home. It is very easy for a young woman to become a television addict, depressed, or extremely bored if she is alone in a house day after day. She needs the companionship as well as the stimulation of having adults and people who care for her around her.

When the husband is away a lot, his time at home needs to be devoted to his wife and his children. To place the additional burden of an extended family on either of you during this time can put tremendous pressure on the marriage. It will also cut into his time with the children. There is already a loss of some privacy when the decision is made to live in an extended family. When the father travels, it takes away even more of this family time. Having a young woman in these circumstances puts additional pressure on the wife as she faces all the decisions that come up during her husband's absences. If the husband is away more than ten days a month, we recommend that you consider becoming a back-up couple rather than taking a young woman into your home on a full-time basis. As a back-up family you would take young women for an occasional supper or evening. Sometimes there would be overnight stays during a weekend or an emergency when the couple who is housing her needs to have some time away.

Leaving Her Alone

There are two major concerns in this area: leaving her alone in your home, and leaving her alone at home with the foster father.

Let's look at the first concern. Leaving the young woman alone in your home is something which must be decided on an individual basis as you come to know her. Some young women are extremely trustworthy and this would not be a problem. With others, you know that five minutes after you leave they will be on the phone and could quickly run up over $100 in long-distance charges. Most young women fall somewhere between these two extremes.

I never plan to leave a young woman alone for the first few weeks. Even if at the interview she seems very responsible, wait two weeks. What you see is not always what you get. Once we feel that we have assessed the situation, we make the decision as to what our plan of action will be. For those young women whom we feel we cannot leave alone, we either arrange time with the counselor, use other support people, or try to find creative ways to allow me to have the time away that I need to run my household effectively. I do try to take the young woman shopping with me as much as possible because I feel that she needs to learn life skills in this important area.

If the young woman is trustworthy, we make sure we have a neighbor or someone available for her in case of an emergency. We always leave a phone number where help can be reached. It is amazing how quickly a baby can come or how quickly an emergency might occur. Generally, I check with the neighbor or friend before I leave to make sure they will be available for phone calls. We have rarely had an emergency, but when we have, we were greatly relieved that we had a system in place.

Now let's consider the other area of concern. Should the foster father be alone in the home with the young woman? We recommend that you avoid this situation as much as possible. Jim and I have always asked the Lord to protect him from false accusations in this area. If something would happen (and the chances are slim), the effects would be devastating. If your children are at home, this is not a problem. Jim would often take a young woman with him when running errands, but he would also take one of our children along too. Let me clearly say that you should not live out of fear in this area, but wisdom is a key ingredient.

Baby-sitting

Should the young woman baby-sit for us? Never take a young woman into your home thinking you will be getting a free baby-sitter. If she is going to baby-sit for you, you should pay her at the same rate you would pay any baby-sitter. When you pay someone to baby-sit for you, it puts you in control of the situation. If there is a discipline problem and you have paid the young woman, you are the employer. This carries much more authority with her than if she lives with you and baby-sits as a favor. Be careful not to overuse her in this respect.

It is also very important to know your young woman well before you allow her to take on this responsibility. There are some young women who have lived with us that I would never allow to baby-sit for us. On the other hand, there have been some wonderful young women who have been a tremendous blessing to us.

Emily was a teacher working towards her graduate degree when she came to live with us. She loved children and had worked with special children. Our youngest child, Shelly, was born with brain damage and has several learning disabilities. At the time when Emily came to live with us Shelly was in occupational therapy, speech therapy, and physical therapy in connection with the handicapped school she was attending. In less than a week, Shelly and Emily had become friends. By the time Emily had her baby, Shelly was going to her each day after school to work on her exercises and homework. Often Emily would have something special planned for Shelly. This was a rewarding time for Emily and Shelly as well, and they became special friends. We have had several young women who have been a blessing to us in this way and we have had some with whom we had to be very careful with regard to their relationship to our children. Over the years, the Lord has protected and blessed our children. He has truly ministered to them, and used our children in ministry to others.

Privacy and Space Needs

As you move into this ministry, privacy will be an issue you will need to consider. As we mentioned earlier (Chapter Two: Your Family), you will notice a change in your own privacy. As you make adjustments in your lifestyle, remember that she needs her privacy as well.

We do not recommend that she share a room with your children. Your children and the young woman both need their privacy. In addition, if the young woman does not keep the room clean, she may, when confronted, say it is your daughter's problem, and make it into a personal "you against me" issue. This problem would never arise if she and your daughter had not shared a room.

I have also found that the young women need time to be alone and to think through their decision-making process. There are a lot of things going on in their minds and they need to have the opportunity to work these through.

If you are considering the possibility of taking in two young women, then they can certainly share a room. They are facing the same crisis and have the same basic decisions to make. If you decide to take two young women, you need to make it clear to both of them that they are not allowed to try to persuade the other one to make the same decision they are making. Jim and I always made it clear that if we ever saw this behavior, a discipline would be required. Each young woman must make the right decision for her and her child. Often when we had two young women living with us one would decide to place her baby for adoption and the other would keep hers. Personally, I thought it was good for them to have each other. Jim and I always enjoyed two young women at one time.

Whether you decide to take in one or two young women, the secret to success in this area is to treat them in the same way you would treat your own children. You allow them to have some privacy and you honor them in this way. At the same time there are certain rules which must be observed and honored. No young woman should be allowed to stay in her room all day. This needs to be made clear at the interview. On the other hand, we never want to be so inflexible as to say that once you were up in the morning you could not return to your room until bedtime. Sensitivity and firmness applied with love are the things that will bring positive results when the issue is privacy.

Emotional and Physical Needs

Smoking and Alcohol

Smoking and alcohol are two very sensitive areas, but they need to be addressed as we begin to build an extended family.

Smoking is an issue which should be approached from a medical point of view. For a long time we thought that only the health of the person who smoked was affected. We have since learned that in cases of pregnancy, the unborn child is also affected by its mother's smoking. Scientists and medical authorities have recently taken smoking one step further and are reporting that even passive smoking is dangerous to the people who inhale the smoke. Passive smokers are people who do not smoke themselves, but live or work in an environment where people smoke.

There are numerous articles available on the dangers of smoking. If you need material in this area we recommend that you ask the ministry or organization you will be working with. They usually have a supply of medical information. If they do not, contact the American Heart Association, American Lung Association or the March of Dimes. Each of these organizations has published material on smoking and its effects.

For these reasons, we recommend that if you do smoke, you consider becoming a back-up couple rather than having someone in your home full-time.

If you do not smoke, we feel you do not need to allow smoking in your home and that it is perfectly acceptable to say that she or her guests may not smoke in your home. Be sure that this rule is in writing in your Family Helps and Hints (see Chapter 10).

Now let's consider the subject of alcohol. Again this is an issue which needs your serious consideration. Some ministries and organizations have already established rules in this area and you will need to abide by their decision. If you have questions concerning the effects of alcohol, be sure to ask your ministry or organization. If they do not have any material, contact the March of Dimes in your community.

I am sure we all have varying points of view concerning the use of alcohol and its place in our homes. Alcohol usage can be considered anything from a glass of wine at dinner occasionally to keeping a liquor cabinet or beer in the refrigerator. Jim and I came from backgrounds where the use of alcohol was left up to the individual, but drunkenness was considered a sin. We would have an occasional bottle of wine in our home and once in a while we had some beer in the refrigerator. Once we got involved in youth work, however, the Lord brought forth the Scripture in First Corinthians 8:9: "Be careful, however, that the exercise of your freedom does not become a stumbling block to the weak." (**NIV**) He also impressed Romans 14:21 on our minds: "It is good not to eat meat or to drink wine, or to do anything else by which your brother stumbles."

Because of these Scriptures the Lord moved on our hearts to remove all alcohol from our home. If we were going to be involved in youth work or have young women living with us who might have a weakness in this area, we certainly would not want to be a stumbling block for them in any way. Because of the alcoholism problem in this country, especially with teenagers

61

and young adults, we personally have come to the conclusion that this ministry requires us to make our homes free from temptation in this area.

Sexually Transmitted Diseases

Most of you will be offering housing to women in crisis pregnancy or to women who have been sexually active. If you are working through a ministry or organization, they may have their own rules as far as sexually transmitted diseases are concerned.

Our response in this area should be one of caution, but not fear. The ministry or organization you work with should have information on the various sexually transmitted diseases. If they don't, you can contact your local health department and they will provide leaflets that will educate you.

Most doctors are equipped to do testing for all types of sexually transmitted diseases. We recommend that each young woman who is being considered for housing be given these tests. We have housed women for well over ten years, some of them with sexually transmitted diseases, but by following the doctor's orders we have never had a problem as far as the safety of our family was concerned.

The important thing is for you to know if the young woman is carrying a sexually transmitted disease. You should know what the disease is, what the treatment involves, and how your family may be affected. Armed with knowledge, you can make a good decision for all concerned. The key is knowledge, not fear.

Doctor's Appointments and Requirements

The doctor's visits and requirements should not be approached simply from a medical point of view. To a great extent, her health care also relates to her emotions and to her spiritual life. Many young women will come to you with fears of doctors, doctor's offices, and blood tests. These fears need to be addressed, but be careful not to be too sympathetic. Going to the

62

doctor and getting pricked by needles are a part of all of our lives from time to time. Remember, if she is pregnant, she may be keeping her baby and her example as a parent will affect her child's future experiences with doctors. If we can help take away some of her fear and allow her to mature in this area, we are not only helping her, but possibly generations to come.

If she has fears or misgivings, talk with her about the doctor. If he is your personal doctor, reassure her about her ability to trust him. Go over in advance what might happen at this visit. If you don't know, call the doctor and see if you can find out what the visit will entail.

Some young women are very good in this area and others actually pass out for no apparent reason. We once had a young woman who hid in the closet whenever it was time to go to the doctor. On one occasion she climbed up on top of the clothes dryer and refused to get off. In moments like this, it took a firm, but loving approach. After we tried unsuccessfully to talk it through with her, we began to impose disciplines. The disciplines increased if she continued to refuse. If we would have had to cancel a doctor's appointment because of bad behavior, we would have called a meeting with her counselor and would have worked out something as a team to keep this situation from recurring. Fortunately, it never went that far.

When the doctor's appointment is over, make sure you have either heard from the young woman or checked with the nurse regarding the doctor's recommendations. If she refuses to follow the doctor's recommendations, again you need to call a team meeting and make a decision as to how to best get her to follow through. Remember, though, to separate the doctor's recommendations into what is essential and what is recommended but not absolutely crucial to her health. For example, if the doctor says to try and cut down on sweets, he or she is not saying this is an absolute, just a good idea. On the other hand if he or she would say that the young woman has shown a trace of a diabetic problem and needs to be very careful, this should be taken much more seriously and needs everyone's cooperation and support.

Personal Cleanliness

This is usually not a problem, but it has come up in our lives from time to time. When this happens we let the young woman know before she comes to live with us that we shower or bathe every day. You can usually tell when there is a problem before she comes into your home. When she meets you for the first time, take note of her personal cleanliness and then let the counselor know that you want to make a few changes in your written rules. I generally do not address this area in our written rules, but add it when necessary.

Another suggestion which seems to help if you notice a problem is to put together a "welcome basket." This basket can contain deodorant, shampoo, bath powder, etc. Tell her to let you know if she needs more supplies. Some of the families we have trained have decided to have a welcome basket for every young woman who lives with them. These baskets can also include a Bible, devotional book, note paper, etc. Sunday school classes or even the ministry or organization you are affiliated with could make a project of providing welcome baskets.

If personal cleanliness is still a problem after all these attempts, then either the foster mother or the counselor needs to take the young woman aside, talk with her, and agree on a course of action. Deciding who should do this task should be a team decision and be made according to the personalities involved based on whom she would best receive from in this area.

Childbirth Classes/Support People

Each ministry or organization usually has some means of providing childbirth classes for the young woman who is staying in your home. Providing childbirth classes is not your responsibility. If no one knows of a resource for these classes, call your local hospital and ask for the prenatal clinic or the maternity floor. They should know the local resources.

Sometimes the foster mother enjoys being the support person for the young woman living in her home. This should be decided on an individual basis. The counselor should be involved in the decision regarding the choice of support person. If you as the foster mother feels that this is not something you would enjoy, that is perfectly all right. There are people who would be happy to volunteer. None of us can be all things to all people. It is important to be honest and to offer yourself only if it is something you truly feel you have the stamina for if it was an "all-nighter."

Transportation

During the young woman's time with you there will be needs for transportation for her. For example, doctor's appointments, childbirth classes, maybe some trips to the counselor or the public assistance office may be required. If transportation is a problem for you, let the ministry or organization you are working with know of your need for help in this area. They often have volunteers who are glad to offer transportation. If they do not have anyone, see if there is someone in your church who might be willing to help out.

I recently had a case where we needed help to get a young woman to her counseling appointments. I remembered a lady in our church who was a widow and had some months ago asked if she could do anything to help. She told me she had a car and loved to drive. We contacted her and she agreed to see to it that Lorie got to all her counseling appointments. During the course of their rides together, they developed a special relationship.

Be aware of your own limitations in this area before the young woman comes into your home. Discuss them with the counselor.

Go over all her possible transportation needs and the options. Usually, if these things are addressed before frustration builds up, they can be worked out with some team effort on everyone's part.

There are a few occasions when the young woman may be employed and need a ride to and from work. Public transportation is an excellent option if it is available in your area. However, there are times when things simply cannot be worked out that way. We had a young woman live with us who worked at a residential facility until midnight. We had to get up very early in the morning and it was simply not feasible for us to be responsible to pick her up every night. We all scurried around and found that there was someone else who worked there who could drop her off at our home. There were only a few times when the ride did not come through, and then we did provide transportation. Be creative, but be realistic in this area.

Another area which needs to be discussed when we talk about transportation is the possibility that she may own a car and want to bring it with her. If you find at the interview that she has a car, you need to set down some rules concerning its use. We have found that the young women who have cars are few and far between so this is not a situation you face very often. Our suggestion for car rules are as follows:

1) If she is employed and needs the car to get to and from work, she is welcome to bring the car and use if for that purpose.

2) Other uses of the car would only be allowed after permission was given by the foster father. This is an excellent way to build up communication between the foster father and the young woman.

3) Your children are not allowed to ride in her car unless special permission is given by the foster father.

4) All expenses for the car are the responsibility of the

young woman. She must show proof of her driver's license and proper insurance coverage before bringing the car to your home. (She should not be driving the car if she does not have proper license and insurance coverage.)

The last area to consider as we discuss transportation is the use of your car. We recommend that she not be allowed to drive your car unless it is an extreme emergency. If an accident would occur, this could cause problems with your insurance coverage. Many young women have drivers' licenses and if you open the door for the use of your car, you will have numerous requests. The result will bring more headaches than blessings.

Insurance

The issue of insurance coverage often arises as couples move into extended family living. There are two types of insurance that need to be considered: homeowners and car insurance.

In thirteen years of living in an extended family environment with over 200 young women, we have never had someone file against our insurance policies nor have we ever been sued. We live in a world that is running scared in this area and often the fear of being sued can keep a couple from moving ahead in ministry.

We urge you to be prepared, but do not live in a state of fear. Most people carry a homeowners' policy. We recommend that within your homeowners' policy you have a minimum of $300,000 of general liability insurance per incident. (Most homeowners' policies automatically carry this amount of liability in case someone is hurt in your home.)Talk with your insurance agent about proper coverage.

The other area of concern is car insurance. Your normal car insurance coverage should cover the young woman when she is a passenger in your car. Again, we *do not recommend* that you allow her to drive your car. Even if she has her own insurance, it could affect your insurance if she had an accident.

If volunteers are being used to transport her to appointments, they should have car insurance and up-to-date drivers' licenses.

Special Occasions

During the young woman's stay with you, you may have the opportunity to celebrate some special occasions. We tried to be very sensitive in this and make these occasions as joyous as possible. Parties were always great self-esteem builders and brought us much joy over the years.

Celebrations

Birthdays were our specialty, and we were not bad at farewell parties, graduations, and holidays. Whenever there is something special to celebrate, we do it! It lifts our spirits and makes our days unique and special. Whenever a young woman living with us had her birthday, we would have a party for her and purchase a gift (up to about $25.00, or within a range of what we did for our own children). Sometimes we would do something special (i.e. pizza and bowling) depending on her interests. When a young woman graduated from high school or received her GED, we celebrated with a graduation party. Often her parents didn't think of this, but we knew how hard she worked. We also provided a gift for the occasion.

Holidays

At holiday times, especially Thanksgiving and Christmas, the young women's family traditions were taken into consideration and blended with ours as much as possible. The dinner menu may have included some of their favorite items. The young women often have difficulty with their feelings during these special holidays because they remember their homes (no matter how deficient in our eyes), and their families. No matter how much you do, their thoughts will be home and sadness often prevails.

On certain holidays we did innovative things. Here are a few of our ideas.

Valentine's Day. One week before Valentine's Day, everyone's name is placed in a hat and names are drawn. The person whose name is pulled is the person they are to express a quiet love for during the next week. This love can be expressed in many ways: making their bed, secretly bringing them a favorite snack, etc. On Valentine's Day, everyone takes turns trying to guess who their "quiet cupid" was. We usually had a special dessert that night as well.

It is a special gesture if the housefather remembers each of his young women (and wife) with a flower, card, or some other special thought. Our children have always loved this gesture from their father and for many young women, it was the first time they had received anything on Valentine's Day.

Family Vacations

Each family has its own style of family vacation. You may be campers, beachcombers, visit family on your time off, etc. If you are planning on taking a pregnant young woman with you, it's good to check with her doctor first to make certain the trip will not be harmful. We have frequently taken pregnant teenagers camping with us, and we have all been enriched by the experience. If she is in her last month and your vacation plans include traveling over three hours away from your hospital, it might be best to make arrangements for her to stay with a back-up couple.

Special Outings

With some families, special outings play a big part in their lives (golfing, bowling, swimming, movies, etc.). Take note of the "What I Like to Do" form to see what outings she might enjoy participating in. Often these events, especially movies, can pave the way for many good devotions and conversations.

Many of today's movies have messages that need to be addressed and this might be a once-in-a-lifetime chance to address them with your young woman.

Other

Pizza, ice cream, and treats such as going to McDonalds can be a form of recreation and can lighten up the entire household when applied properly. We all need a special treat now and then, sometimes for no reason except that it would be fun for all.

Board games, jigsaw puzzles, etc., can be a great source of recreation for the young woman and your family. Game night can be a regular part of your devotional program. Play games or work puzzles with the young woman. There is so much interaction that can take place during these activities. Many times she will open up better in this environment than any other place.

Listen as you work or play. Take note of what is being said. You may hear things which are causing her great pain and indicate a need for healing in her life. Like Mary, the mother of Jesus, ponder them in your heart. Don't reason with her immediately or make the conversation too heavy. Be gentle and, as the Spirit leads, carefully guide the conversation.

Crafts

Crafts are wonderful self-esteem builders and help take up hours which might otherwise be filled with nothingness. When the young woman comes into your home, she should fill out a "What I Like to Do" form (see Appendix). On this form is a list of crafts. Take the time to help each young woman get started in some craft activity (even if you have to learn it yourself!). There are often people in the community who are very gifted in this area and may come to your home to teach her. As you meet people, develop a resource list of their gifts, and as each young woman arrives who is interested in a particular area, contact that resource person. The one-to-one contact is ideal because it makes the young woman feel special and valuable. The end product of the craft project is worth much to her. Praise her and display it if at all possible.

Rosemarie was living with us. She always came across as one who appeared to have it all together, yet she was distant and cold. One day I had a friend come to teach us how to do macrame. I let Rosemarie know that we would be learning this special craft the next day. She promptly informed me in no uncertain terms that she "did not do crafts."

I kindly, but firmly told her that my friend was coming especially for her, in order for her to have something to do during the day. I told her that I wanted her to be polite and to make an effort. If, after my friend left, she decided she was no longer interested, we would look for something else. I made it clear that she was not going to spend the rest of her time with us simply doing nothing.

When the next morning arrived, she did everything she could to get out of spending time with my friend. Finally, I had to get her and tell her we would work together. My friend had brought enough material for both of us, and so we began to do macrame. I had never attempted this before myself, so we were both new at it. Rosemarie began very begrudgingly, but as the hours went by, she got into her task more and more.

Within a week she had finished her macrame project and had completed mine as well. She asked if we could go to the store and get more material. A couple of years later I visited her home and she took me to her room. It was filled with things she had made. She thanked me that day for making her try. She said it gave her the courage to try other crafts as well. There was no question that crafts had been a big step toward building her self-esteem.

Many young women who lived in our home discovered areas of talent that they were not even aware of, and continued to develop their abilities in these areas well after they left our home.

Respect and Belief in God's Ability

The most important thing to remember as you build your new family unit is the need to respect and believe in each other. The young woman needs to be respected as much as she needs to respect you. She also needs to believe in you and she needs for you to believe in her. Don't be blind, but believe in God's best. Sometimes we live or work with someone for days or weeks and see no apparent response, or the response we do see is not what we think it should be. One of the secrets to this is patience: a God-given patience causes us to put more trust in God than in ourselves. God created her and He does have a beautiful plan for her life. You are a stepping stone to the fulfillment of that plan.

7

Spiritual Issues

We cannot tell a starving man about the love of Christ and expect him to listen until we have fed him. The same is true of the young women who come to live with us. Once we have supplied their basic needs, the environment is set up for them to receive all that Christ has for them. In order to set up an environment that will allow them to hear, feel, and care about the Lord, we need to look at several different areas.

Church Attendance

If we had asked the young women who lived with us if they would "like" to go to church with us on Sunday mornings, forty-eight out of fifty would have said "no." I firmly believe Sunday morning service should not be an option, but a requirement.

Many of the young women who will live with you have never had a positive experience with "religion." Many will have attended church at some time, but I found that most had some negative experience that had affected their view of Christianity. Because of this experience, they are not willing to give Christianity another chance. By making church attendance a requirement, you may be opening the door for healing for them. As they sit in your church and feel the love from the people in your congregation, as well as from you and your pastor, it will begin to make a difference.

It is good to invite your pastor and his wife for dinner at your home soon after her arrival. She will do much better meeting and getting to know your pastor in this environment than if you take her to some function at the church and introduce her. Although she may be in your home several weeks before the pastor will be able to come for dinner, having him visit will have a positive effect on her feelings toward him and your church. Our pastor would drop in a few times a month and many of the young women who lived with us developed a very special relationship with him. This is one of the reasons why it is important to talk over with your pastor your call to this ministry. Having advance notice will give him time for education and preparation for ministry to your unique family. If the young woman is from your community and presently attending a church, there is generally no problem with her continuing to go there. Transportation to her church should be her responsibility. If she is unable to get transportation to her church, then you might want to call her pastor for her and see if he could work something out.

Sometimes we had Catholic young women living with us. Since we were not of that faith, we would make arrangements for their transportation and on occasion take them to Mass either on Saturday night or early Sunday morning. Then they would attend services with us. This worked out very well.

There are many young women today who are born-again Christians because they were "forced" to go to church with us on Sunday. I remember the young woman who, several years after leaving our home, wrote and told us that she had made a commitment to Christ through Campus Crusade in college. In her letter she shared that they (Campus Crusade) thought they "had gotten" her, "but it was really you who got me years ago." It is important to remember that we are often seed planters, but we do want good ground for our seed. That ground is prepared and plowed by the Body of Christ.

Participation in Church Activities

If you are a family that goes to church on Sunday morning, Sunday night, and Wednesday evening on a regular basis then you need to make this clear in your written rules ("Family Helps and Hints"). It is perfectly acceptable to make this a rule if it is something you do on a regular basis. You need to make these activities and requirements very clear. The young woman will then be given the option of deciding whether she can handle all the extra "religious activity" or not.

If you are a family that goes to church on Sunday morning, but makes a decision weekly as to whether you will attend church on Sunday evening and/or Wednesday evenings, then you need to be more flexible with her. If you find that she is trustworthy and can be left at home alone, then you might want to be more lenient about requiring her to attend extra services. If she cannot be left alone, she will have to abide by the decision of the family. As a member of the family, she needs to be allowed to have input into the decision, but the final say will be yours.

If your church has a youth group and/or singles group, you might want to suggest that she attend and see if she enjoys it. If you are going to offer this, make sure you have checked with the youth leaders before sending her. It is very difficult to go to a new place, much less a new church and be asked to walk into a new group. Often the youth leader will be willing to come and visit her or have one of the young people from church invite her to come and pick her up for the first meeting. We have had young women really get involved in youth or singles ministries, including attending retreats, etc. Their participation has instigated life-changing experiences for the group as well, as the group has been able to address issues they had never considered before.

On the other hand, we have had young women who simply did not do well in a group environment. Make these types of decisions on an individual basis rather than through an overall rule.

Our family attends a home group while our teenage daughter goes to youth group. This is a regular part of our family life. Because of this we allow the young woman to choose between going to home group, youth group, or singles group, but when everyone in our family goes, she goes as well. As our family situation changes, so will our rules.

Family Devotions

What are devotions? How important are they? Devotions provide an opportunity to guide, counsel, and direct. They provide space and time to interact as a family in a supportive environment. Devotions are a time when a living example of the true Christian life is allowed to come forth in an atmosphere of love, trust, and acceptance. Everyone is drawn into this love when it is a place where total openness and freedom to be yourself is permitted. Devotions are a time when you can share with each other your pain and your joy.

Our family devotions usually took place Monday through Friday of every week. It is best to plan devotions ahead of time. This allows for a continuous of themes flow throughout the week and more is accomplished this way.

We held devotions after dinner, but the time depends on the household and the day. Some households prefer a set time every night, while others like some flexibility. We recommend you make family devotions a priority. We found when devotions were not a priority, our household began to lose its closeness.

Devotions can be fun or serious. They can deal with every area of life, including some very practical needs. Vary your devotional presentation and subject. They can be times of tremendous growth for the young woman and for you.

Some excellent resources which we used to plan our evening devotions are:

Dad's Magazine, PO Box 340, Julian, CA 92036;
Group Magazine, Box 202, Mt. Morris, IL61054;
Penny Power, Box 2859, Boulder, CO 80321;
Youth Specialties, 1224 Greenfield Dr., El Cajon, CA 92021
The Serendipity Materials, available through most Christian bookstores.

We also used television programs, Christian and secular videos and tapes, board games (such as the Ungame, Roll a Role, etc.), or current events as a starting point for our devotions. Through them, we tried to show how Christianity touched all aspects of life, and that building family could be instructive and/or fun for all those involved.

According to authorities concerned with youth and drug abuse, the two most detrimental factors that lead to alcohol and drug abuse are a lack of self-esteem and boredom.

As we look at the young woman in your home, it is highly probable that low self-esteem helped lead her into her present situation. The experience of living in a Christian home allows time for the young woman to develop to her full potential. She most likely needs love, understanding, attention, and a sense of belonging. She needs to feel liked and worthwhile. Devotions help this process to continue. If she does not increase her self-esteem and sense of worth, she may remain promiscuous if she thinks her need for love can only be achieved through sex.

Begin devotions by explaining what is going to happen. We feel it is important that the parents participate in the devotions, rather than simply leading or "teaching." There is no secret agenda in devotions. The goal is to build a supportive family where love, trust, and acceptance are paramount.

We need to impose some rules, though. Everyone learns from the start that interrupting, probing, giving advice, and judging are not allowed. We should all reap the fruit of listening as well as being listened to, caring as well as being cared for, loving and being loved, and affirming as well as being affirmed. The success of devotions can best be determined not by how much the family is enjoying themselves or growing spiritually, but in its acceptance of each other.

The entire devotional experience should lead to a new experience, first for the young woman, and second for you as you learn and develop your creativity. Remember, if God would be blessed through devotions, He will supply the right ideas and creativity. Your responsibility is to make the time.

There are three basic parts to our being — body, mind, and spirit. Our spiritual lives are of utmost importance, but they must be nurtured and encouraged. You cannot force someone to love Jesus. Oh, yes, the right set of circumstances and pressure can make someone say a prayer of salvation, but only a yearning for God and a heart of repentance will bring true salvation and peace. Our goal should not be to say that everyone who has lived with us has received salvation, but rather to say that everyone who has lived with us has been exposed to a loving and caring God. Hopefully, seeds were planted that will eventually lead to salvation and peace.

8

Finances

Never let your concern over finances keep you from becoming an extended family. If you need a little help in this area, most of the ministries and organizations you are working with can help out in some way. Sometimes crisis pregnancy centers start a small food bank that extended families can draw from. If you are involved in a church and finances are keeping you from serving as an extended family, let your pastor know your need. There may be a means within your church for families to help support you while you support the young woman.

Extended family living can become an important ministry for your entire church. There is so much that people can do to be involved. They can help financially, provide food, transportation or maternity clothes, be support people, teach crafts, help tutor the young woman, etc. It is a joy when the church family pulls together in a ministry of this type.

Household Expenses

Sometimes our finances are affected when we chose to live in an extended family. When you take a young woman into your home, your budget may increase in a couple of areas. Generally when you add one more person to the food budget, you may notice a slight increase in the weekly food bill. Another area in which you might see an increase is your electric bill. Our electric bill never increased more than $5.00 a month with each girl, but we did sometimes notice an increase caused by the additional electricity needed to blowdry hair, heat hot water for showers, open the refrigerator a few extra times, etc.

Room and Board

Should you expect her to pay room and board during her stay? This needs to be evaluated by the ministry or organization you are working with and by her counselor. They will take the following into consideration:

1. If the young woman's parents are involved with her, are they able to offer any financial help? It is important that parents be as much a part of the planning for their daughter as possible. Some parents request housing for their daughter because they feel there is too much emotional pressure on the entire family. In many cases, these parents are able, and may contribute to their daughter's room and board.

There are other cases in which the parents are not able to, or refuse to help. If they are truly unable to help out financially, then certainly the daughter would be housed free of charge. If they refuse to help, then the case needs to be carefully considered. There are some parents who are "users." They will use everyone they find who will give them a free ride. Sometimes, by putting a little pressure on them, they become more responsible. This is important for their daughter. When she knows that her parents can help and will not, it definitely affects her respect for them, and makes her feel she is of little value to them.

2. Is the young woman receiving public assistance? In most states, when a young woman is receiving welfare, she is required by law to pay some sort of room and board. We

recommend that one-fourth of her public assistance check be turned over to the family for room and board.

3. Is she presently employed? If she is employed, she should also contribute one-fourth of her income for her room. This helps her to be realistic about the cost of living. We do not help young women by totally paying their way when they have some funds of their own. This promotes a way of life that says "The world owes me a living." Even if you are financially able to house her for nothing, make sure you help her be responsible in this area.

If you do not need room-and-board payments, we suggest you contribute them to the ministry you are affiliated with. There are many wonderful couples who may need assistance in order to have a young woman in their homes. Your center could channel your room and board payments to a fund to help families who require some extra help.

Budgeting and Spending Money

If your young woman is employed, she should have help to work out a budget if she does not presently have one. If she is unemployed and on welfare, then she should be budgeting her money. This budgeting help could be offered by either the family or the counselor who is working with her. We have found that this is an excellent area in which to involve the foster father. It gives him a chance to communicate with the young woman. In either of these situations, you cannot control her money, but you can guide and direct her.

Even if she does not work or is not eligible for welfare, she should have a small monthly allowance. Everyone needs some money to work with and there is no way that we can judge her responsibility in the financial arena unless she has an opportunity to work with some funds. If her parents are able, the counselor could ask them to contribute her allowance. We recommend that she receive thirty to forty-five dollars a month.

If the parents are unwilling to provide an allowance, then the ministry or organization you are affiliated with should help you. Sometimes a church or Sunday school class will take on the ministry of supplying allowance for a young woman each month. It is not your responsibility to give the young woman spending money of any kind.

Budgeting is very important. It is especially important when the young woman is considering keeping her baby. The counselor needs some way to see how she handles her finances. If she has the opportunity for budgeting sessions and is given the funds to work with, responsibility or irresponsibility will show itself. If she blows all her money on record albums, makeup, etc., the counselor can address the need to look at her ability to meet the financial needs of raising a child. if she is considering keeping her child. We have had young women do very well in this area and have been delighted with their ability to budget. Some have walked out of our home with a small nest egg. Others have spent every penny they have received as soon as they got it. They would even ask Jim or I for an advance of funds. **never give out advance allowance unless it is an absolute emergency**. If you do this it teaches them that "someone will always bail me out. Someone will always take care of my problem." We have worked with parents who have spent years buying their children out of one problem after another, only to have the problems increase over the years rather than diminish.

Medical Expenses

All medical costs are the responsibility of the ministry and/or organization that places the young woman in your home. They have the responsibility of making it clear to the young woman that **you are not responsible** for her medical expenses.

She will need vitamins and possibly some other medications during her pregnancy. Meeting these expenses as well as the expense of the Childbirth Classes, etc. should be the responsibility of your ministry or organization. They may choose to have the young woman and/or her parents take on the responsibility for these costs, or they may take the responsibility themselves. There are often doctors in a community who are willing to donate free vitamins. Some ministries and organizations provide free childbirth classes. There are numerous ways to meet this need, but you should not be one of them.

Other Basic Needs

Haircuts and makeup are also special needs for young women. I have never had a problem getting someone to style the young women's hair. There has always been a hairdresser in our church or community who has been willing to cut, style, and on occasion even give a perm to the young women who lived with us. This is an excellent way for hairdressers to use their gifts in ministry.

There may be times during the young woman's stay with you when she might need a pair of shoes, a coat, maternity clothing, etc. If the young woman living with you has clothing needs, let the counselor know and together you can work out how to meet this need. She may have some resources of her own. If she is employed or is receiving welfare you could help her budget a portion of her funds for such items. If she has no financial means at all, the ministry or organization you are working with may have clothing available for loan. Some churches and other resources in the community are able to provide clothing free or at very inexpensive prices. To help teach her how to stretch her dollar, you could take her shopping at "almost new" consignment shops, or a Goodwill store.

Once again, her clothing needs are not your responsibility. You may have people in your church, a personal friend, etc. who would like to bless her in this area. Certainly this is acceptable.

Years ago when we first began to live in an extended family, we had a young woman come to live with us named Maria. She brought very little clothing with her. We had managed to meet her needs for basic maternity clothing, but now the time for the baby's delivery was drawing near. We needed a robe and nightgown for her hospital stay. Our local hospital at the time was always very warm and so it was essential that we have a summer robe and nightgown for Maria, even though it was in the middle of winter. As we looked into our usual resources, we found that there were no summer outfits available.

Maria became concerned and we agreed that we would make this a matter of prayer. Each night during our devotions, we prayed for a nightgown and robe for her. One evening we went to church and when we arrived home there was a beautiful, new, mint-green robe and nightgown set to match laying on Maria's bed. Maria's robe and nightgown fit her perfectly and they were a perfect color for her. She was thrilled and she knew that God truly cared about her and her unborn child. To this day we do not know where this beautiful set came from, but we do know that God hears and answers prayer.

Over the years, we have learned that it is important that we commit everything to the Lord. We have found that when we do this, He will give us a resource to secure it, give us the finances to purchase it, or every now and then we will be the recipients of a special miracle. If Jim and I had chosen not to live in an extended family environment, think of all the miracles we would have missed!

9

Mealtime, Food, And Nutrition

Mealtimes are an important part of our lives. This chapter will include the mealtime experience, the menu planning, grocery shopping, table manners, dinner-time fellowship, and proper nutrition. The above considerations affect not only our eating habits, but our emotions and health.

As extended families we have a wonderful opportunity to teach many life skills. Dinner times can be an example of why the Lord provided the need for food. A glance at the Scriptures shows how mealtimes with Jesus were times of fellowship and encouragement. He ate with sinners to encourage them and chose mealtimes to work many of His miracles.

We, too, have experienced many miracles during mealtimes. There have been times when we were living in an extended family that I opened the oven door and said, "Lord, You did it to the loaves and fishes, please do it to the chicken." Our budget was limited, so many times I would have less than I needed to feed my growing family, but the Lord was always faithful. We did all we could, and then He worked a miracle.

Over the years we have learned many practical things that have helped make our mealtimes more enjoyable and our preparation time more fulfilling and life-teaching.

Make mealtime a happy time, full of conversation and praise. There are times when discipline must be rendered at the meal table, but try and keep this to a minimum. If possible, wait until the meal is over and then take the young woman aside and confront her concerning her bad behavior. Many of these young women have never experienced mealtimes with a family or often have only had bad experiences from family members (i.e. yelling while eating, slaps across the face, etc.). Indigestion is a problem for us all and stress and anxiety can promote this problem. Pregnant women automatically have a greater problem in this area. We need to be sensitive to this at all times and not to push too hard, especially when it might affect her physically. If you find you are having a meal in total silence, there is a problem in the family. Mealtimes should be times of fellowship.

Table Behavior

Lay out the rules for table behavior. A good way to do this is to have a devotion focusing on table manners. Or, you can add a section in your Family Helps and Hints. It is important that you emphasize caring for others (i.e. passing food, not taking the last piece without asking others, etc.). It is also important that you lay out the way you want mealtime to go (instructions on setting the table, how you want clean-up handled, how you want the cook to put the food on the table, etc.). If this behavior is not followed, take the young woman aside and make it clear again. If it is still not followed, then discipline is in order. Try not to give out discipline at the meal table in front of others. It is always best to do it privately.

Some young women are gifted in the area of cooking, some in planning meals; some in both, some in neither. When the young woman comes into your home, it helps if she has filled out the form "What I Like To Do, What I Do Well" (see Appendix). This will give you an idea of her cooking ability and shopping skills. Use this form as you guideline as to how much help she is going to need.

Kitchen Projects

Menu Planning

Planning a menu can be another time of building family. There are several ways to do this and each family will develop their own method. Try to show her how the use of recipes, food groups, and finances play a role in menu planning.

Shopping

Let the young woman help you with the grocery list and sorting coupons. A good project for her is to be responsible for coupons — cutting them out, sorting, and throwing out expired dates, etc. This life skill will help her tremendously as she starts her own independent life or later marries and raises her family.

Taking the young woman shopping for groceries is an excellent way to teach shopping skills and to have mother/daughter sharing. You may not want to do this every time, but include her a couple times a month. Each young woman should experience this life skill during her stay.

If you can, try to keep to a minimum the times you run to the store for odds and ends. Try to develop a means that will allow you to grocery shop once a week, making extra trips the exception. This will help her develop planning ahead skills and help her learn how to make what you have least until the next shopping trip. There is also the cost of gas, time, etc. to be taken into consideration. All these things need to be taught as life skills to help the young woman manage her money, and help her learn to plan ahead instead of living impulsively.

Cooking Projects

Cooking projects are good for learning to cook and for building self-esteem. An afternoon of baking or some other cooking project is a great way to build your relationship with her. Sometimes a volunteer can be brought in to teach something special (i.e. baking bread, cinnamon rolls, cake decoration, etc.). Be prepared for complaints as you work through some of these areas. Complaining is typical, but is more evident when self-esteem is low. The purpose of complaining is to prepare the way for failure. "If I don't succeed, I didn't want to do it anyway." If your projects move on in joy, there will be successes and as the self-esteem is built, the complaints will diminish. Instead of allowing the complaining to get to you, lift it before the Lord, asking him to heal her and to use you as a vessel.

Gardening, Freezing, and Canning

Garden times, including freezing and canning projects, are good opportunities for lift lessons, helping to build family and to teach the young woman to make the best of things that are necessary but not always fun. Try to keep the atmosphere light during these times and a reward (i.e. pizza, ice cream, a swim, etc.) is often a great way to end.

Weight Gain

The desirable average weight gain during pregnancy is approximately twenty-five pounds. If the young woman stays within the range of twenty to thirty pounds, she will provide for the growth of her baby as well as the changes in her body that support and protect the baby.

It is best for her to gain a small amount of weight each week. Ideally she should gain one pound a month for the first three months. From the fourth month on she should gain three quarters of a pound each week.

If a young woman is overweight, do not allow her to diet without the doctor's permission and instructions. Do not take a young woman to any weight-loss organization (i.e. Tops, Weight Watchers, etc.) without the doctor's permission.

Pregnant women need approximately 300 more calories a day than they did before pregnancy. These extra calories are best supplied by such foods as milk, sandwiches, puddings, etc. A pregnant woman does not need to eat larger portions of food when she is pregnant.

Nutrition

Each young woman should drink six to eight glasses of water or other fluid each day. (This is the same amount that is recommended for adults each day.) Four to five of these liquids should be milk with Vitamin D. If she cannot drink milk, this should be discussed with the doctor. Milk can be consumed through pudding, soups, cereal, hot chocolate. One-half cup of cottage cheese and one-half cup of ice cream equals one third cup of milk. Milk should be offered at every meal.

Two servings of protein are needed each day. Meat, fish, poultry, eggs, dried beans, peas, nuts, cheese, cottage cheese, and peanut butter are some of the sources of protein. Eggs and/or meat should be offered at each breakfast. A protein should be offered at both lunch and dinner.

Whole grain breads and cereals provide fiber which is a natural laxative. Raisins and sometimes popcorn help when constipation is a problem. Fruits and vegetables are very important during this time and help keep the young women from needing laxatives. Do not give a laxative without a doctor's permission.

Five to six servings of whole grain or enriched breads, cereals, and cereal products are necessary each day during pregnancy. Check the labels on breads and cereals to make sure they are either made with whole wheat or whole grain or are enriched with minerals and vitamins.

Fruits and vegetables are an important part of a diet during pregnancy. There should be a fruit at each meal and at least one vegetable at lunch and two for the evening meal.

I found that over the years our family's own nutrition improved because of living in an extended family. We became aware of making our mealtimes enjoyable and have treasured them over the years. Many of the young women who have lived with us have commented on how much our mealtimes meant to them. They have thanked me for the cooking projects and have reminisced over our times in the garden together or the times we were up to our elbows in peach juice.

One of the young women who lived with us showed some interest in cake decorating. Since this was not a skill I had, we arranged for her to go to an adult education class in our community. A friend of ours went with her and they became good friends. Today she is married and earns extra income from her cake decorating business. On our twenty-fifth anniversary, she brought a cake for us that she had made and decorated: her gift of love to us for our gift to her years ago. The cake was beautiful and I will treasure its memory always. Surely, God uses many varied ways to bless us and to help bring wholeness to others.

10

Family Helps and Hints
(Rules)

There are boundaries within each of our households. When Jim and I became parents, our parents had a major influence on us as we set limits on our children. We received additional instruction in parenting through our walk with the Lord. After we came to know Christ, we made it our practice to lift our need for rules and disciplines before Him and to seek His guidance. We have used the Bible as our guide for establishing order in our home. This does not mean that our rules were inflexible or could never be adjusted, but until they were changed, they were respected and followed.

Before a young woman comes into your home, she should be given your written rules. We like to call ours "Family Helps and Hints." When she arrives to stay, you should go over them with her again and ask her if she has any questions. If not, it is assumed that she understands the rules and agrees to abide by them. Of course, it is important that the rest of your household follow the rules, too. If your family does not follow the rules, the result will be confusion on everyone's part.

Everything we do affects everyone else. As parents, we must set the example. If we don't follow the rules, and enforce them with our own children (depending on their ages), we can't expect the young woman to respect them or follow them. This does not mean that the father is only allowed to talk on the phone for ten minutes, but it does mean that you both honor the spirit of the rules as they have been set forth, and follow them to the best of your ability.

For the young woman, each boundary (if crossed), or each rule (if disobeyed) carries its consequence or discipline. You want to establish the concept that you are not just suggesting good behavior in your home, you are requiring it. Bad behavior carries penalties. Some of these penalties should be prescribed in your "Family Helps and Hints." Others will need more flexibility and should be at your discretion.

The purpose of the boundaries, besides enabling you to live together and besides encouraging respect for authority, is to teach life lessons. Once these life lessons are learned and the level of behavior is acceptable, the boundaries "seem" to disappear and no longer remain issues. She will have achieved "freedom with responsibility" and will have become a contributing member of the family.

Over the years we have developed a basic set of rules "Family Helps and Hints" (see the Appendix). With each young woman we may make adjustments, additions and/or deletions, but this has become the foundation from which we build.

Write It Down!

We instituted written rules in our household for three reasons. First, it is important to remember that teenagers and young adults do not respond well to a lot of verbal commands. As our children got older, we found it was more effective to use our conversation for encouragement and praise as much as possible. By putting the rules of our household in writing, this kept us from having to use verbal communication to give orders, assign chores, etc.

Another good reason for written rules is that they will cut down on your level of frustration. It is frustrating to know that you gave a specific instruction, yet be told that you never said anything!

Third, I came to understand that many of the young women we lived with wanted to do a job the way I wanted it done, but simply couldn't remember it all. The written rules and instructions were the answer!

If you have a certain way you like for your laundry to be done, don't just run through your instructions verbally. I suggest you write or type it out on a piece of paper. I created a standard worklist with instructions beside each job. I have rarely found an adolescent or young woman who thinks that cleaning a bathroom includes wiping off the soap dish or replacing the toilet paper. They just don't think of it. So over the years, I've learned to spell out the tasks. If you have certain products you want used, put them down in writing as well (i.e. "clean the tub, sink, and countertop with Comet, wash out the soap dish, use Vanish in the toilet bowel, mop the floor with Spic N'Span, check the toilet paper and make sure there is an extra roll on the back of the toilet" etc. etc.—whatever is the norm for your household). We hang our worklist on the refrigerator, and if there are any questions the young woman or family member can easily refer to it. I can't tell you how many confrontations we've avoided just by putting things in writing.

Some time ago I got a call from a couple who had a young woman living with them. They had been to our seminar and were using many of our suggestions. "We have a problem. I wonder if you can help me," the mother started off. So I asked her to tell me what happened.

"Well," she said, "I got ready to leave today and I asked Carol if she would clean the bathroom while I was out. She said, 'Sure, no problem.' When I got back several hours later, I went to use the bathroom and when I sat down on the toilet I noticed it was all sticky. Then I felt the sink. It was sticky, too, and so was the tub! Something's wrong here. What do I do?"

I suggested that she go to Carol and without making it into a big deal simply ask her, "Tell me about how you cleaned the bathroom." Then see what she says.

The woman called back in a half hour. "I found out what happened. She dusted the toilet seat and sprayed furniture polish all over the tub, the sink, everywhere! She sprayed so much, that even dusting it didn't get it off, and everything got sticky. Now that I know the problem, what do I do about it?"

I suggested she go into the bathroom, shut the door, and reclean everything. Then the next time she gives Carol the bathrooms, give her some instructions with it. "Do you know what I would like you to do this time? I'd like you to take this Comet and sprinkle it in the tub and scrub it with this sponge," etc. etc. In this case, it all worked out okay. Carol's self-esteem was preserved, and she learned how to clean a bathroom in the process.

Housekeeping

One of the things which happens when we take someone into our lives is the possibility of false guilt on our part. This seems to be especially true for the mother in the family. She may have a tendency to feel guilty about asking the young woman to do a chore which she normally does herself in the daily routine of housekeeping.

We need to recognize the need for the young woman to have some household duties. These chores help teach responsibility and life skills. They also help keep her busy during her stay with you. A pregnant young woman is able to do any housework that a married pregnant woman would do. The only time she should not be required to do housework would be on orders of her doctor.

For the "non-favorite" chores, I recommend everyone involved in the housework share the chore on a rotating basis. Worklists are ideal if there are more than two people doing the housework (see Appendix for sample worklists). Be creative in your worklist and remember to make it clear what each job entails.

Worklists can be done on a weekly or daily basis, depending on how often you clean your home. It helps if you have a method for everyone involved to check off the chores as they are completed. This enables you to keep track of what still needs to be done and helps you know what you need to check if jobs have not been completed. We usually cross off the jobs we have completed.

Three of our standard rules address household chores:

1. You will participate in the daily tasks of housekeeping, cooking, laundry, etc.
2. Your bed shall be made by 10:00 AM
3. You will do your own laundry, including your towels and sheets. We do ask that you try to have a full machine. If the washing machine is not full, please ask to see if there are a few additional items that could be added.

Now let's talk about laundry. Her laundry arrangements should be worked out on an individual basis. Whether you both share laundry responsibilities or she does her own laundry, it should be picked up daily from the laundry area and put away. If she doesn't collect the laundry, we would confiscate it and then let her buy it back from us at ten cents per item.

The system worked well for our extended family, and also worked for our children. I have one daughter who would dress out of the laundry basket every day if we allowed it. She hates closets or the thought of putting clothing away. We keep a jar and all the clothes money we receive after collecting ten cents per item goes into the jar. When the jar fills up, the family goes out for pizza or some other treat.

General Rules

Our general rules covered several areas such as bedtime, mealtime, lying, etc. Rather than have a separate category for each, we decided to make a general category.

Bedtime

1. Bedtime is 11:00 PM unless special permission is given.
2. Wake up time is 8:30 AM unless special permission is given. You are to be dressed and ready for the day by 10:00 AM
3. If you are going to be in your nightgown in the evening or in the morning before 10:00 AM, you must wear a robe. You are not allowed to get into your nightgown in the evening before 7:00 PM.

You can work bedtimes and wake-up times anyway you want, but we found you need to have set times to wake up and go to bed. As much as possible, try not to let her stay up after you go to bed. This does not mean you never go to bed and leave her up, but you want to avoid her staying in bed until afternoon and then staying up until 1:00 or 2:00 in the morning. She needs to mold into the routine of your household as much as possible.

It is also important that you be aware of the amount of time she is sleeping during the day. If you find she is taking more than a two-hour nap each day, it is possible that she needs more activity or that she is having problems with depression. Often when we are very upset or hurt, we try to sleep our problem away. Generally,when she sleeps so much during the day, it means she is not sleeping well at night. Make the counselor aware of any special problems in her sleep habits. It is important for her to get enough rest, but it is also important for her to keep her mind and body active.

Nightgowns and robes are an issue that need to be clearly stated in your rules. The young woman will appreciate your letting her know the rules beforehand. Families are all different and whatever the routine is for your family should be the routine for her, especially in the area of attire.

Mealtime

1. We eat dinner together as a family. You will have some responsibility in meal planning and preparation.
2. We eat what is set before us unless there are special medical needs. As a family, we try to vary our meals to allow for everyone's favorites from time to time.

As discussed in Chapter 9 (Food and Nutrition), mealtime is a special time. It is important that you have some basic statements in your Helps and Hints so she knows what to expect.

I tried to avoid everyone eating separately as much as possible. In our home, dinner was always a family meal. We generally had lunch together, even if there were only two of us. We usually had leftovers or sandwiches or salads for lunch and would help each other get it on the table. Breakfast was much more flexible because I was getting children off to school. The young women would usually get her own breakfast unless she was up and about as the children were going to school. When that occurred I would fix her breakfast with the children.

Sundays were always rushed, but we had breakfast together as a family. We had our big meal after church and everyone got his or her own dinner later in the evening.

These things worked well for us. Each family is different and you must set your Family Helps and Hints up to match the character and routine of your family. There is no question that living in an extended family helps us to evaluate many areas of our family's lives and maybe make some changes for the better.

Personal Cleanliness

You need to have a statement concerning this in your rules. A statement such as "We bathe and shower daily, but are careful about the use of water" is sufficient. It covers the person who might not bathe enough as well as the one who might want to spend the entire day in the shower. (See also Chapter 6: Personal Cleanliness).

Transportation

A rule concerning the use of your car needs to be included in your rules. This avoids verbal conflict at a later date. You may want to expand the rule to include rules for her if she has a car of her own and is bringing it to your home (See Chapter 6: Transportation).

Lying

Lying is a serious problem for many people. Another problem is exaggeration. We need to be aware of this in our lives as well as the lives of the women we live with. The Bible is clear about the use of our tongues and how much trouble they can get us into. You need to make a clear statement in your Family Helps and Hints that you will not condone lying. Some disciplines we have used for this offense in the past have been:

> Dishes for a week
> Loss of privileges
> Looking up a word in the concordance and writing out every Scripture that uses that word (i.e. truth, honesty, love, etc.)

It is often hard to catch someone lying because they will deny that they said a certain thing or try to turn the situation around so it looks like they were an innocent victim. I always ask the Lord to give us discernment and to make the proof obvious.

One time we had a young woman who we suspected had been writing to her boyfriend against her parents' wishes. She was sneaking out and mailing the letters. We confronted her, but she denied the whole thing, and there was no way we could prove who was right and who was wrong.

We went to the Lord and asked Him to reveal the truth to us. Within a week one of the letters she mailed came back. She had put the wrong house number on it. (We never permitted the young women to get the mail out of the mailbox. This allowed us to see what types of mail they were receiving and also it helped with our own privacy.) Because of this rule, she was caught red-handed! We now had a letter addressed to her boyfriend in her own handwriting.

We talked to her about the importance of telling the truth and we talked with her counselor as well. We talked about her boyfriend and honoring her parents. He was allowed to call and knew the number. The counselor talked with her parents and we were able to have her boyfriend visit our home on a few occasions. This accomplished two things: one, we were able to deal with a bad trait in her life lying; and second, we were able to open up the doors of communication more for her, her parents, and her boyfriend. She did the discipline we gave her and thanked us for our understanding.

Medical

Smoking, Drugs and Alcohol

1. If you are caught with alcoholic beverages, or using or possessing drugs not prescribed by your physician, you will be asked to leave our home within twenty-four hours.

2. Smoking is prohibited while at our home. This rule shall be observed by all members of our family and their visitors. The first offense shall receive a warning, second offense will have dishes for a week, third offense will have dishes for two weeks. A fourth offense is a decision to leave our home.

Some medical issues need to be addressed in your Helps and Hints. It is important that you make very clear statements as to where you stand on the use of alcohol, drugs, and smoking. You will notice that in our sample Family Helps and Hints, we not only give the rule but the end result. All three of these areas are important to the life of your family as well to her life and the life of her child. (See also Chapter 6: Smoking and Alcohol.)

Doctors' Appointments and Childbirth Classes

You shall attend childbirth classes, go to doctors' appointments, and follow their recommendations.

This issue is addressed in depth in Chapter 6 under Emotional and Physical Needs. It is always good to make a statement such as the one above in your Family Helps and Hints. This makes it clear from the beginning that you are committed to her health and well-being. If you have problems with her in this area you need to talk with the counselor and work out a solution as a team.

Religion

1. You will attend church with us or attend a Christian church in our community on Sunday mornings.
2. You shall have the opportunity to participate in other church activities and services in the community.
3. Blessing will be said at each meal.
4. You will be required to attend family devotions.

Once again, it is important to mention that you need to develop your Family Helps and Hints according to your family's routine. Obviously if you do not have family devotions you would not have a rule concerning them. Try to keep your statements general, yet clear. For example if you have devotions two or three times a week but they are sporadic, then the statement above is perfect for your family. You have said clearly that when devotions are held, she will attend. If you get too specific and then don't follow through, it sets a bad example. Why should she complete a task or assignment or follow up on her commitments when you do not honor the Family Helps and Hints that were given her? Never include anything in your Family Helps and Hints that you will not follow up on. (Also see Chapter 7: Spiritual Issues.)

Visitation

1. Your parents are welcome in our home with the understanding that they will notify us twenty-four hours in advance and work out arrangements for the visit with us.
2. Other relatives and friends will be allowed to visit on the same basis as your parents. If your parents have an objection to a visitor, this will be given serious consideration on our part.
3. Boyfriends will not be allowed in our home in the absence of the foster father.
4. You will not be allowed to go out with friends and/or relatives without our approval.
5. Visits home shall be arranged with us. These visits shall not occur more than twice monthly or until you have been in our home for three weeks. Once visiting arrangements have been made **they may not be changed,** in the middle of a visit except for extreme circumstances.
6. You will not be allowed to stay out all night with anyone other than your parents unless special permission is given.

7. No boyfriends shall be allowed Monday through Thursday during the school year, if you are in school or studying towards your high school equivalency test. Otherwise boyfriends will be allowed to visit at our discretion.
8. Dating will be regulated and arranged according to your situation, your parents' input, and our approval.

You do want to welcome and get to know the young woman's parents if at all possible, but this does not mean they should be allowed to come and go in your home as they please. When we plan to visit any friend, unless they are very special people to us, we usually call ahead. Her parents should honor you in this way. On rare occasions, it might not be convenient for them to come at the time they have chosen. Do not feel you need to rearrange your schedule to match theirs. Certainly there will be times when you might want to rearrange the schedule for some special event for them, but make this the exception rather than the rule.

It is equally important that her parents honor the visiting arrangements as far as her visits home are concerned. Before we made the rule about visiting arrangements not being changed, there were many times parents or the young women would call us and ask to stay an extra day or come home a few hours later. Very often we had been out on a Sunday and had gone out of our way to be back home in time to receive her. On some occasions, our entire family had given things up in order for us to be home for her. This would cause resentment to build between her and our children, which, in turn, put pressure on us. We found that this rule helped her and her family plan ahead, and it certainly helped us as we arranged our time around her time away. (See also Chapter 11: Parents, Boyfriends and Friends.)

School

1. If you have not graduated from high school, you shall attend school or study towards your high school equivalency test.
2. You shall be allowed to participate in any school sponsored activity according to your physical ability, if your grades are average or above.
3. If you are maintaining below an average grade in any school subject, you shall be required to attend study hall for the remainder of the marking period and/or until the grade is raised to average or better. Study hall shall be held at the dining room table and shall consist of one hour of study per subject per day, except Saturday and Sunday.

You would make these rules part of your Family Helps and Hints only if you are receiving a young woman of school age or one who will be working towards her high school equivalency diploma. I highly recommend that you make working towards a high school diploma a requirement for living with you. Many of the young women who lived with us had been high school drop-outs and would never had received their diplomas if we had not had this rule.

We often had friends who were willing to help them in certain subject areas, and there are also adult education courses in every community to help young people study for their high school diplomas. This will mean so much for their future! You can work with her counselor as to how the schooling will be achieved, but it definitely should be given a high priority.

Good study habits were very difficult for many of the young women who lived with us. Because of this we would actually set up times of the day to study. For example, if she were a morning person we would have study time in the morning and she would do her chores in the afternoon. Everything was to be completed by dinner so that the evenings could be a time of rest and relaxation for us all.

Phone

1. You shall be allowed to talk on the phone for fifteen (15) minutes. You must ask permission to make phone calls.
2. No phone calls shall be made or received after 10:00 PM
3. Collect calls will not be accepted unless we give special permission.
4. You will not be allowed to call boys, but they are welcome to call you.
5. You will be responsible for paying for any long-distance phone calls you make.
6. Misuse of any of these phone rules shall result in the following disciplines: First offense will receive a warning and the rule will be explained. Second and ongoing offenses will be given three days of phone restriction for each offense. (No calls in or out, except for family contacts which will be limited to ten (10) minutes during the time of discipline.)

Our philosophy is that the telephone can be an excellent vehicle for teaching responsibility, sensitivity to others, and self-discipline. Asking permission to use the phone is done for two reasons:

1. It reinforces one's responsibility to others. We are reinforcing the practical application of loving one's neighbor and respecting authority. Most young women just do what they want without regard to the feelings of others.

2. It enables the foster parents to be aware of "all" that a young woman is doing. The Spirit guides in this.

Most phone abuses occur when a young woman first comes to live with you. She will need to be gently reminded at first, followed by firmer discipline when unwillingness to cooperate ("I forgot") is evident. When a young woman has a bad day she tends to use the phone more. The phone is also a means for sharing her struggles with the outside world. The hospital is another time of extensive phone use because of her elation and depression.

We recommend that she not accept any collect calls without your prior permission. However, you can encourage her to call collect. When she first arrives, she can run up a gigantic phone bill and leave your home before the bill comes!

Someone always challenges our rule concerning the young women not calling their boyfriends. We received more flack from the young women about this rule than about any other rule we ever made! Our society tells young women that it's okay to chase young men. We were told that we were old-fashioned, that today, everyone calls their boyfriends, etc. Jim and I held firm in spite of all the verbal abuse, and today many of the young women who lived with us are grateful for it.

So often we'd hear from a young woman how much her boyfriend cared for her. But we noticed she would call him again and again; he would rarely call her. This "fantasy" of hers led her to continue to make plans as if he were very much in the picture when this was not the reality at all.

We finally decided to be firm on this issue. When the young woman first came for an interview we made the rule very clear. We told her that God made the boy to be the "chaser" and her to be the "chasee." We explained that, in the years to come, it would be important for him to know that he won her, not that she trapped him. We made it clear that he was welcome to call her and that we hoped he would come to visit us. She could certainly write to him, and we hoped he would write back.

105

Again and again we watched young women come to the reality of their relationship. The young men would not call or they would call so sporadically that she would know that he was not as interested in her as she was in him. This was very painful, but we tried to be loving and encouraging to her. We were grateful that she was with us and had a support system around her when the reality hit. Only when she came to grips with the relationship could she move along with her plans for herself and her child.

It is hard to believe how something as innocent and helpful as a phone can be so destructive and instructive. We see this as one of the basic learning tools in a young woman's transformation to being sensitive to others.

Television, Tape Players, Radios, Stereos

1. All radios, stereos, tape players, etc. are to be off from 12:00 midnight until 9:00 AM

2. If your stereo, radio or tape player is found playing in an empty room, it will be confiscated for three days.

3. No television shall be allowed in your bedroom.

4. Stations, volume, and time of listening are at our discretion. No earphones are allowed. Misuse of this privilege will result in confiscation of the radio, stereo, or tape player for one (1) week.

5. Records and tapes shall not be brought into our home without our approval.

6. Television shall be turned on only during the hours of 5:00 PM until 11:00 PM on Monday through Friday (except by special permission). On Sunday, the television may be turned on after morning church service and remain on until 11:00 PM. Television may be monitored by us. Misuse of this privilege will mean the loss of television privileges for one (1) week.

It is important to set rules in this area. Some of you may not want heavy metal or non-Christian music in your homes. If that is the case, you need to make that clear in your Family Helps and Hints.

We found that many young women had never been exposed to contemporary Christian music. They believed that all Christian music consisted of hymns. We made sure that there was a tape player in the young woman's room. We only allowed Christian music to be played in the main part of the house and we tried to get tapes the young women would enjoy. We also played Christian music exclusively in our car. After a time, many would ask permission to take certain tapes to their bedrooms. As special occasions arose, they would ask for Christian tapes as gifts. We found it a wonderful way to expose them to today's Christian music.

Many of these young women are TV addicts. They would spend the entire day in front of the television if you allowed them. It is important for her to understand the environment she is coming into. If she refuses to come to your house because you do not own a TV, or because of your TV rules, that is her choice. We don't allow TVs in bedrooms. We don't see a need for them. We believe it is a bad habit to have a TV in your bedroom: it takes away from some of the intimacy of the bedroom and when a whole family is involved, it pulls the family apart to have everyone watching television in a different place. As a rule, TVs in bedrooms just do not build family unity.

It is also important to set some rules on what is allowed to be watched. Jim and I use the three "s" plan. Our family is not allowed to watch anything super sexy, super violent or super-natural. We have always reserved the right to change the channel.

Another area of concern we have is soap operas. Many women today are addicted to them. At one time in my life, I planned my day around "General Hospital". When I came to grips with my addiction, it was very difficult to break. If this is a part of your life, maybe it is an area you need to examine. Many of the young women who lived with us begged us to give in on this area. I told them that if they could list five good things that watching a soap opera would do for them, we would reconsider the rule. No one ever came up with five good things that soap operas do for people. This is a hard statement, but we are in the business of making people whole and wholeness does not come by filling our hearts and minds with immoral behavior.

Discipline

In spite of the best efforts, there are times when discipline needs to be applied.

Types of Discipline

We prefer using disciplines that are basic, and yet firm. We have used chores for discipline more than any other method. We especially like giving dishes, kitchen floors, and bathrooms as discipline because they are generally chores that young women do not like to do.

We have also taken away privileges as a discipline (such as phone privileges or television privileges) but we have found that the young women prefer housework to loss of privileges. Unless the infraction is serious, the only time we generally take away phone or TV privileges is when a rule has been broken in that specific area.

Rebelliousness and Defiance

What do you do when you have a young woman in your household who absolutely refuses to do what is expected of her? In other words, she openly defies you.

Is she misbehaving because she is testing your love for her? Does she misunderstand the rule? Does she want you to "kick her out"? Does she want you to think she is tough or cool? The boundaries should remain firm, but you can let her know where you think "she is at."

Should you back down because you see her need for help more than she sees her need for rules? After all, shouldn't we meet her where she is, even if it's a state of rebellion? Where do you draw the line? We hope the following guidelines will help in choosing a constructive course of action that will not compromise the standards of your home.

Let's say you have a young woman who has broken a rule more than once. You have given her a discipline, but she refuses to comply. In other words, she dares you to make the discipline stick. Be sure that you are assessing the situation correctly. Realize that defiance is the exception rather than the norm. Most young women, after some initial grumbling, will comply when the time comes. If she is truly defying you, what do you do?

First, if counseling services are available, contact her counselor, explain the situation, and work out a plan of action together. If after talking to the counselor, the young woman has not changed her mind, be sure you talk to the counselor again. Postpone the discipline or consequence until you take this step. Everyone involved should be in agreement.

Second, recognize that if you want to minister to "all" her needs (not just housing), you want to minister in line with the Scriptures. The Bible teaches that actions and choices result in consequences: "For whatever a man sows, this he will also reap," (Gal. 6:7). Jesus said, "And you shall know the truth, and the truth shall make you free," (John 8:32). If you give in to her or try to protect her from the harsh realities of life, you are not ministering truth to her.

Third, recognize the challenge to authority. Often, she may not have had a good authority figure in her life so she is going to test you to see how you measure up. The real issue is not the discipline or consequences of the broken rule, but rather, who's going to be in charge.

Fourth, talk to her in a peaceful, gentle way. If you have prayed that God would send you the young women He wants to your home, tell her. Tell her she's not there by accident, but that God brought her there because He has a special plan for her. Tell her Jesus loves her, wants the best for her, and wants to help her with her situation. Assure her of your love.

Remind her that she knew the rules and expectations before coming. Wherever she goes, she'll have to come under some form of authority: home, work, church, or government. Remind her that part of growing up and maturing for all of us is accepting the authorities over us and cooperating with them. Also, mention that God works through authority to show us His will for us. Then give her a chance to reconsider.

Fifth, approach the situation from the point of view that she has two options. Either she chooses to accept the consequences of her action, or, by refusing to accept the consequences, she chooses to leave your home. There is no middle ground. Explain the two choices, but **always** keep the situation in terms of *her making a choice*, not you forcing her to leave or rejecting her. She either freely chooses to come under your authority or not.

The sixth thing you have to do is follow through. If she chooses to accept the discipline, you administer it and go from there. If she decides to leave, it does not mean she does not need your help: it just means that she is not yet ready for it. Until she is ready to receive what you have to offer, she cannot benefit from it. If she cannot handle the authority structure you have set up, there's a serious question as to whether she will benefit from anything else you have to offer. Nor does her decision to leave mean you have failed. There will be many others who can benefit from your home.

Part of follow-through involves helping facilitate her plans for leaving. Contact her counselor immediately and have her arrange with the young woman for her departure. Her parents may come to get her that day, or she might be taken home. She may need to go to a shelter or to a friend's home. This is not your responsibility. She knew the consequences and now she must live with them. Try to make the arrangements in twenty-four hours, or forty-eight hours at the most. This will be healthier for her and your household, rather than postponing the departure.

After she leaves, it would be helpful to plan something together as a family, some activity that will take everyone's mind off the experience: bowling, a movie out, etc. It brings finality to the situation. It's over—life will go on.

And what of the effects of all this? How was it positive and constructive?

For the young woman leaving, the effects will generally be very healthy as long as you keep the whole thing in the realm of her making the choice to stay or leave. You wanted to help her, but you did not take away her freedom of choice. She will respect you in the long run for not pulling any punches. You dealt with her on the basis of reality and the Scriptures, and did not let her "use" you.

The effect on the rest of your family members will be healthy, but there will be an adjustment period after she leaves. Make it clear to all that it was her choice to leave. It will be a good learning experience of the "sowing and reaping" principle.

The effect on you is that you will feel more established in your position. Even though you did not want her to leave, you will have peace that you respected her freedom of choice. Also, you will know that you followed through on your word.

As far as the effect on others, hopefully they will express their support for you and encourage you. You can inform others of what you are doing, but you have to do it. And when you do what you have to in a loving but firm way, you come out a little taller, and a little more confident and established in the task to which the Lord has called you.

Family Meetings

Family meetings can be especially important when you have someone outside your family living with you. The family meeting is a time when family matters are discussed, plans made for the weeks ahead, and special love and encouragement given to one another. There are several ways to use a family meeting.

You can set a time once or twice a month when the family gets together. This could be in place of a normal devotional time that your family participates in.

You can have the family meetings at random whenever a need arises. (Sometimes this may have to happen when a crisis or special problem occurs, even though you work on the basis of a regularly scheduled meeting.)

A major topic for a family meeting should be your family's plans for the weeks ahead. The young woman with whom you live has had so much crisis in her life already that one of your goals should be to help add order to it. Surprises are usually not welcome. To know the family activities in advance makes her feel more secure. When discussing future plans, make sure that everyone knows who will be involved in the outings and activities. Will this activity be something everyone will participate in, or is it optional? Include your own plans as well. You can announce that mom and dad are going out for the evening on such and such a date.

If a special problem occurs in the family or a rule needs to be changed, a family meeting is an excellent time to discuss these areas. Be sure there is a clear understanding of why the rule is being established, abolished, changed, etc.

Another reason for a meeting is what we like to call our "complaint night" or "truth session." This is a time when everyone joins together and airs their complaints in the open (providing they concern more than one individual). The problems

112

are discussed and solutions suggested. One exception is when two people have a conflict with each other. This should be worked out privately according to Matthew 18:15:

> And if your brother sins, go and reprove him in private; if he listens to you, you have won your brother.

When these meetings are a regular part of your family, it allows you to say to people who complain regularly, "Why not consider bringing your complaint up at the next complaint night?" This helps cut down on day-to-day complaining and allows people a way to vent their concerns. Some great ideas come out of these nights; hearts can be softened, and love can be predominant.

Family meetings build unity. It is important that each person feel valued and that they feel that their opinion is wanted and, in fact, needed.

We hope that your family is encouraged and challenged by the thought of establishing your procedures and writing down your "Family Helps and Hints." There is no question that within the home comes the bottom line of all that we say by way of how we live. We really must live what we believe. Being a parent is demanding and life-changing for all!

11

Parents, Boyfriends, and Friends

Parents

We who are involved in extended family living can be assured of one thing—for every young woman who is pregnant and unmarried, there will most likely be a set of hurting, grieving parents. Some will be struggling under the heavy burden of despair and hopelessness; others will be self-condemning, certain that they have failed their daughter. They are all generally "crushed in spirit."

How can we, while caring for their daughter, also strive to be a "healer and a lifter of their heads"?

We've found that there are three types of parents. The first is the rejecting parent. Sad to say, your involvement with this parent—and the young woman's involvement—will probably be minimal. These are the parents who refuse to be part of the entire situation and constantly reject their daughter when any form of communication is attempted. It is likely that this crisis and/or problem pregnancy is only one of many crises in the family, and that the entire family structure is under great stress and upheaval. It is often understandable that they are unable to deal with an additional crisis. You, therefore, have a great responsibility to this young woman, as you are truly her main support system. You must be prepared to walk through many painful times with her, constantly encouraging and comforting her. This type of family structure provides great opportunity for you to go to the Source of all comfort, Jesus, and pray for the healing of relationships.

The second type of parents are the ones who reject initially, but later come to an acceptance of their daughter's situation. This is the type of parents you will most often deal with. Often, their acceptance simply comes with time. You can be of tremendous help in enabling this acceptance to come about by just being there to listen, encourage, and support. You must be willing to walk with them through their pain. Be careful not to jump to any conclusions during their time of rejection. They are probably overwhelmed and need the healer of time to bring their emotions into right order.

And the third parents are the accepting parents. These parents have been able to love unconditionally from day one with no thoughts of rejecting their daughter. This is not to say that they are not hurting, grieving people. They, too, are in need of our support.

How can we as extended families use our God-given gifts to minister to these hurting ones? First and foremost, pray for them. Before any parent conference or visit, pray together as husband and wife and pray with the young woman's counselor that God will minister to their needs through you, and that you will be open to the direction of the Holy Spirit. Ask the Lord to love them through you. Expect the best of them—this helps release faith that God will work out the best possible solution for them in this situation.

Parent conferences or visits are wonderful times for ministering to the parent. After all, this should be their time—an opportunity to have the freedom to "dump." Be assured that all parents will approach their first parent conference or visit with some fear and trepidation. They're wondering what you're really thinking about them and their "failure" and whether you will accept them.

So, it's up to you! Be warm, accepting, and positive. Welcome them into your home with a smile and handshake or hug. Offer them a cup of coffee and just spend some time "chit-chatting." Show compassion and warmth. Remember that focusing your attention on them will help them feel loved. They will know you care. Use eye contact. Don't let yourself be rushed. Let them know you realize they are hurting and that you are there for them.

It is good to open and close in prayer if you are having a parent conference. This can be such a special time, particularly for Christian parents. It is also a testimony to the non-Christian parent of the loving God we serve. We might well be their first introduction to the Master. If the parents have come for a visit, a prayer at the end is often well-received.

Remember that everything will not be accomplished in the first conference or visit. It is just a beginning. Attempt to have them express their feelings; how they're doing, how they feel about their daughter and the baby, etc. There may be much pain and inner feelings to deal with. Share your faith that God is in the business of bringing good out of a bad situation and making a way where there seems to be no way.

One type of parent who definitely needs our support is the parent whose daughter releases her baby for adoption. Their grieving is intense—often even more intense than their daughter's. This is their precious grandchild, and in many instances, their first grandchild.

You can serve these parents by letting them know in advance what to expect. The counselor can be a great help in this. They need to realize that even though they feel that the adoption plan is the best option, they will still experience a period of mourning. This is normal!

As the young woman's time of delivery draws near and the decision for adoption has been made, her parents need to be prepared for her hospitalization. What are her expectations from her parents? Does she want them to see and hold the baby? take pictures? Is it her desire that they be active participants in the celebration of a new life?

And what of her parents? What are they feeling? Many will express to you that "whatever our daughter wants to do is what we desire. We will be there for her." Others will wish to visit their daughter in the hospital but will not want any involvement with the grandchild. And there will be a few who will not even be able to visit their daughter during her hospital stay. The pain is too much to bear. The counselor should help the parents with most of these questions, yet sometimes it can be a blessing to share parent-to-parent.

It is at times like these that we can step in — temporarily —and be for the parents and for the young woman what her parents are unable to be at this time. We can be celebrants in this new life.

It is very important that these decisions and expectations are talked through before the time of delivery. The young woman needs to voice her desires and give her parents the freedom to respond as they are able.

Whatever the final decision, we're not called to judge. We are called to minister God's love and acceptance to them.

Remind them that you will be available for them. Often they will simply need a shoulder to cry on. Some parents will be blessed by having other supportive family members and/or a pastor to help them through this time. For others, you represent all the support they have.

Through this, our source of strength is Jesus, a "man of sorrow, acquainted with grief." He yearns to comfort them when they mourn. Many times, He will use us as the vessel through which to comfort. What a privilege we have!

Boyfriends

Boyfriends are a subject all their own. We found that only about three out of every ten young women who lived with us had boyfriends that related to us in any way. Although the numbers were small, they were challenging and filled our lives with joy. Jim and I could write pages about boyfriends! Some are attentive, others are completely out of the picture. And some will show up periodically or later on in the pregnancy. Let's look at the three types:

Attentive

The attentive boyfriend can be good and/or bad for her. If he truly wants the best for her and the baby, he will be an asset to your efforts, but he may often have problems of his own. He needs your friendship and love as much as possible.

If he is unrealistic and demands things of the young woman, you need to gently, lovingly, and firmly show him the realities. An example of this type includes the young man who insists he and the girl are going to get married, keep the baby, and live happily ever after. The reality may be that he is a high school dropout, working at a gas station, and still living at home. You will not be able to change his mind, but you can hope there is enough time until the baby is due for time to be the teacher. The counselor can give them tasks such as making a budget, hunting for an apartment, etc. By the time the baby arrives, reality may have surfaced. Don't put their ideas down. Use your communication with them for encouragement and praise as much as possible.

Ben was one positive example of an attentive young man. He lived in a rented room, worked in a gas station, and was going to high school. He wanted to be responsible, but he had no money. He and Susie had agreed on adoption and planned to be married after they finished high school.

Ben came to Jim and asked him if there was some way that he could take some responsibility for Susie. Jim worked it out with Ben that he would come over on most Saturday afternoons and they would work around the house together. During this time Jim and Ben built a special relationship. I still remember Ben with great fondness and love.

Out of the Picture

When a boyfriend is no longer a part of the young woman's life, she will feel rejected. Her self-image is usually lower than the young woman who has an attentive boyfriend. She blames herself for believing in him.

Don't tear her friend down, but help her to see the positive points about the situation. As Robert Schuller once said in a sermon: "Any bad situation can either make you bitter or better." Point out that: 1) next time she will be a better judge of what she wants, and 2) what if they had gotten married and he had left?

Often, the young woman with no boyfriend is much easier to live with. But be sensitive to her feelings. She may act as if it doesn't matter, but in reality she may feel forgotten, hurt, and rejected.

Periodically In and Out of the Picture

The boyfriends who are here today and gone tomorrow or who turn up late in the pregnancy are the greatest problem.

Although they have been physically removed, in reality they have been constantly keeping an eye on the situation or else they would not keep involving themselves.

Many times they make demands or promises which make things extremely difficult for her. When they show up or call after a long silence, she is so happy that it is hard for her to be realistic.

Marylou had lived with us for several months and during that time her boyfriend had made only one contact very early in her stay. As the months rolled by, she completed eleventh grade, made a plan for adoption, and had begun to look at colleges. Things were going so well! Finally labor day arrived. It was a long labor and I went home to get some rest. Later in the day I went back to the hospital to see how she was doing. As I walked into the room I saw a huge bouquet of flowers and a big box of candy. It was evident by the look on Marylou's face that she was delighted.

She couldn't wait to tell me that David had come to see her. She had called one of her friends about the baby, and the friend had let David know the news. He had brought the flowers and candy, had apologized for not calling, and had asked her to marry him. "Isn't it wonderful?" she beamed. "Now I will keep the baby and we will live happily ever after."

I couldn't believe what I was hearing. I just knew that the young man had shown this sudden interest out of guilt and was not going to follow through. I also knew that there was no way I could convince Marylou of that.

This was a time for quick thinking and keeping my emotions under control, even though I was feeling angry, hurt, and sad for her. Marylou was a very feminine person so immediately I asked her if she would like to have a wedding? I told her we could have a wedding gown made, we could plan a little reception, and after they had some marriage counseling, we could arrange for a special wedding.

121

How her eyes lit up! She thought I was going to try to talk her out of their plans, and instead I was building on her dream. I told her to invite David to visit her at our home when she got home from the hospital. In the meantime we agreed that it would be best for the baby to go into foster care as originally planned. She could then work out a new plan with the counselor.

She came home. David called a few times, and never came to visit. The pain for Marylou was intense, but she was forced to face the reality of her situation and we were there to support her. It wasn't long before we stopped hearing from David entirely. Marylou did eventually place her child for adoption, finished high school, graduated from college, and is now married.

I think the key in these times of crisis and pain is not to overreact, but to be sensitive to her feelings. On the other hand, it is important that we do not make it so easy for her that we literally force her to keep moving in a direction that will later destroy her. Jim and I have always taken these special circumstances to the Lord and He has been a great blessing to us.

Let me repeat some of our basic rules to help you as you learn to love and live with boyfriends:

Telephone limits (ten to fifteen minutes per call);
Young man calls young woman, not vice versa;
When visiting, he must be a gentleman at all times;
All dating and visiting arrangements are to be made through the foster father;
The boyfriend should not come to the house when the foster father is away.

Visiting and Dating Arrangements

We have found that the best way to begin a relationship with a boyfriend is to take him and the young woman aside on his first visit. Make it clear you are glad he has come to visit and that you care about him. Make sure he is aware that there is counseling available for him. If he seems open in this area, either give him the counselor's name and number or ask the young woman to work out arrangements with the counselor so that he could come to some of the sessions. Make it clear what the boundaries of your home are. We never allowed boyfriends in the bedrooms!

Right away they may ask you about dating. We always made it clear that we would make that decision after we had had a chance to get to know him better. It was rare that we ever allowed a young woman to date while she was in our home. Once in a while when Jim felt they could be trusted, she might be allowed to go to a movie and then to get a sandwich, but Jim would always want to know what movie and would ask questions when they arrived home.

The argument you'll hear most frequently is, "After all, he is the father of my child, we have been dating a long time, and you can't cage me like an animal." We would respond that it was obvious to us that their dating record had included some irresponsible decisions. As a result of these decisions they were now both facing many problems concerning their future and the future of their child. We always made it clear that he was welcome in our home and that it was not our desire in any way to break them apart.

Our experience over the years has been that the majority of the young women who lived with us eventually matured, and the young men did not. During her stay with us, the young woman would come to realize that he was not what she wanted in a dating and marriage relationship. A few of the young women continued to date their young men and an even fewer number married.

Occasionally when we would call the young man to responsible behavior, he would simply quit visiting and would stop calling. This was very painful for the young woman, but it would have happened anyway and would probably have caused her even greater pain had she not been in a supportive environment.

Boyfriends are people too. They are unique and special in the eyes of God. Some are troubled and will not receive from you. Others will rejoice at finally having found someone who cares.

Husbands of the Young Woman

If the young woman is married or has been married, her husband presents a special set of circumstances. In today's society a young woman could be married at fifteen and divorced or separated by seventeen. In many of these cases the husband is out of the picture completely and this pregnancy is to another man. If, in some cases, she still has contact with her husband, then we believe that the following needs to be considered:

If they are divorced, we should treat the ex-husband in the same way we would treat boyfriends. He is no longer married to her and therefore there is no reason for him to have special privileges.

If they are separated, then we believe it should be a requirement for living in your household that he be seeing a counselor or pastor. His pastor or counselor should then contact the young woman's counselor. If they are one-and-the-same then your direction in this area will be from the counselor. If there are two counselors, the young woman's counselor should be the one who communicates with you. This communication should cover the stipulations as far as visits are concerned.

My recommendation to young women who are separated is that they need to be willing to go to counseling themselves and insist on their husbands seeking counseling. Only when the counselors say that they should talk with each other, visit each other, or go back together should that be allowed within your household.

The reasons for this is that so often these women make decisions based on feelings. She begins to feel lonely and scared. She thinks there may never be anyone else, so she had better stick with him. He begins to say how sorry he is and may even send gifts. Some even say they are going to church and everything will be different. Only a counselor or pastor can discern whether they are ready to be together again. We should honor their counsel.

It should never be our intention to break up a marriage. Our hope is that the couple will get the help they need and healing will occur. If this happens the possibilities of a healthy marriage and good parenting are possible. If not, the problems will continue to arise, but this time there will be children involved. We have an excellent opportunity to offer the help that needs to be offered, instead of simply putting a Band-aid on a problem that will occur again.

Friends

Often friends can put pressure on a young woman. Some friends have very definite opinions in one area or another regarding:

> adoption vs. keeping the baby
> marriage vs. breaking up
> religion
> parents (yours and hers)
> people in authority
> school and jobs

Friends, like boyfriends, can either be an asset or a liability. If they are the type who "doubles our joy and divides our grief" they will be a blessing. Sometimes it can be meaningful to include this friend in some of your family's activities.

Other friends can be a problem. If they are opinionated and have problems themselves, it can cause additional problems for the young woman. Don't discredit the friend, but instead try to teach the young woman about real friendship. Like the young men, her friends also need limits.

In many of these areas, your counselor can be very helpful. It is important as we deal with all the different people in her life to see them as children of God, no matter what their present circumstance. Each young woman has been created by Him and is loved by Him. And so are her parents, her boyfriend, and her friends.

12

Adoption Verse Keeping

When we decide to become an extended family, there are issues we need to deal with that we may never have considered before. Most of us never had to work through a decision about placing a child for adoption or keeping our child. Most of us were married by the time our children were born. Therefore, we have no idea of all the thoughts, facts, and feelings that are part of this important decision for any young woman who is pregnant and in crisis.

When a young woman becomes pregnant, questions, fears, sadness, joy, and most of all confusion may overtake her. Since she cannot escape the reality of her pregnancy, it affords an opportunity for her to stand still and deal with her pregnancy in a mature manner. She must also stand still long enough to look at herself and become reacquainted with the person she is and is becoming. This may be the first time she has even had to evaluate her life.

A pregnant teenager has four choices concerning her pregnancy: abortion, marriage, single-parenting, and adoption.

This will be one of the most important decisions any young woman will ever make. She is totally responsible for another person's life and yet she has so many needs of her own. Since we feel clear that abortion is not an option according to God's Word, that leaves us with three choices. In this chapter we will discuss marriage or single parenting as one choice (keeping) and adoption as the other.

As foster parents, it is important for us to be educated concerning both decisions. Our job is not to help her make the decision about the baby. This is the counselor's responsibility. But we should be informed, supportive, and be prepared to be good listeners. She may often ask you the question: "What do you think I should do with my baby?"

My response to this is always: "I am really praying for you in this area. I know this is a very important decision and I am asking God daily to direct you,I know that you love this child. I also believe I can trust you to make the best decision for you and your child. There are two other things that I know for sure. One is that if you truly seek God's will, He will direct and guide you. Two, I know that the God I love and serve is not one who helps one and hurts another. For this reason I know that if you put the child's life first and seek God's will, He has a decision that will be best for both you and your baby, not just for today, or next month, but for the rest of your life."

Today we have resources available that we didn't have five years ago to help young women with this important decision. We have workbooks (*My Baby and Me*), books, trained counselors, and families like you. All of these resources help a young woman move towards a good decision for her and her child.

There are a couple of things to consider in this area. Each of us have our own personal feelings about adoption and keeping. We are all opinionated. We can't help but be. We have been influenced by the people we have known, the media's presentation of this subject, and the books we have read. If you are an adopted child and your adoption was a good one or you have

128

adopted children, you will probably be strongly in favor of adoption. If you were a person who became pregnant, married the father, and have lived happily ever after, you will probably feel that keeping is the answer. There are those the young woman knows who are so opinionated that if she does not go their way, they will be disappointed in her and will let her know that she is making a mistake. It is so important that we remember this is her life and she must be the one to make this important decision. If you use your influence to persuade her one way or the other, she will never take responsibility for the decision herself. This will harm her, as well as put a barrier in your relationship.

Let's take a look at the options.

Keeping

Young women who choose to parent their children most often include, 1) young women from a cultural background which tends to raise children collectively; 2) young women who have had previous abortions, if the abortion was forced on them by their parents or another person: 3) young women who have had bad experiences with adoption; and 4) young women who need to be loved and think this child will provide all the love they need. Not all women keep for the wrong reasons, but many do. We have had some wonderful mothers live with us and we have had young women who made it obvious to all that they were not ready to parent.

Whether a mother keeps or places, she will experience pain. If a young woman places for adoption, the pain is immediate and intense. She will never forget she had a child, but the pain will subside, and if she has been allowed to grieve properly she will feel good about her decision in time.

When a young woman keeps her baby, she first experiences joy, but the pain comes as single-parenting or marriage becomes a reality. In both cases, pain will be experienced (as in all our lives) but at different times and in different ways. You will have to help prepare the way for the young woman who is keeping, under the direction of her counselor.

The counselor will take the major responsibility for this as she helps the young woman work through her decision. You may be asked to help by taking the young woman shopping after she has planned a week's menu so she can price the items out. These times can be special times between the two of you.

We had many situations in which the young woman wanted to keep her child but had nowhere to go. She would ask if she could stay with us. Consider carefully before allowing the young woman to return to your home with her child! Over the years we found that it was better to provide the young woman with another setting outside of our home if she was planning to keep the baby. In most cases, when she knew from the start that bringing the baby to our home was not an option, she would find a resource. In cases where she had no resource, there was another alternative.

The Christian adoption agency in our area offers one month of free foster care for any child. During that time, the mother may visit with the child and yet would not be bonded to the child if keeping did not develop into a reality for her. Again and again we found that the majority of women who used this type of service eventually placed their children for adoption. If we had allowed them to bring their children into our home, they would have become bonded to them and the inevitable separation would have been far worse for both the birthmother and the infant.

During the time the child was in foster care, the mother continued to live with us. Sometimes we would allow the mother to stay with us for an extended time after the adoption or while she was working through the keeping process.

We are not saying you should not under *any* circumstances allow the mother back in your home with her child. There may be an occasion when the mother had a realistic plan and only needs a place to stay with her baby for a week or so. In this situation, by all means let her come back, but only if she needs very temporary housing and everything else is in *definite* order.

For the young woman who is keeping her baby, the hospital is a time of both joy and concern. Now she has made her decision and parenting is upon her. She needs to be reassured and yet also allowed to state her fears and concerns. Flowers are always in order when a child is born because it is a time of celebration.

Adoption

Very often, someone asks, "Why would anyone choose adoption?" Young women who choose adoption do so because they have put much thought and prayer into this decision. I have never had a young woman place a baby for adoption who didn't love the child. In every case, the birthmothers chose to grieve for the sake of their children.

Today, young women who make a plan for adoption may send things with their children. They are allowed to send letters and to express to their child why they decided on adoption. They may also send a letter to the adoptive parents making special requests, within reason. The baby's grandparents may send a letter with the child, if they desire. Let me share a letter which was written by the grandmother of one of our young women to send with the child in his new home:

Dear precious one,

I am writing because I am your grandmother and I wanted you to know how very much you are loved by your natural parents and their families.

While comforting your mother through the adoption proceedings, I told her that relinquishing you was "the

131

*greater love" and that the greater love is always "sacrificial."
And of course we know whenever we must sacrifice, it costs
us something. We saw your life as an "unpolished jewel";
and yes, it was at great cost that we gave you up. But wisdom
embraced us and gave or caused us to know that whenever
the sacrifice is for the right cause, the end result — product of
the sacrifice — shines forth as bright as the sun! That is our
confidence for your life!*

*As I held you in my arms for the last time, I committed your
life to the Father's care and keeping, knowing that He had
hand-picked your adoptive parents and that you were
entrusted to the care of those who would love, nurture, and
help bring to perfection our "unpolished jewel." So, dear
angel child, we have a perfect assurance that your life, care,
and happiness are in the Great Master's hands and the end
product of our sacrifice will be your life — a "gem of great
price" fit for the Father's use. Amen. Our love is always with
you!*

Your Grandmother

*P.S. "For this cause I also suffer these things; nevertheless I
am not ashamed; for I know Whom I have believed, and I am
persuaded that He is able to keep that which I have
committed unto Him against that day." (2 Tim. 1:12)*

No longer do we have children who know nothing about their
birthmothers or grandmothers.

Preparing for Grief

Tom Dodge, who was a housefather at the House of His
Creation, a Christian maternity home, gave the following
thoughts in a paper he did for a class on Pastoral Care of the
Dying:

"If a mother is likely to choose adoption she needs to be prepared in much the same way as the adolescent who is going to keep her baby. Her identity needs to be strengthened so that she can feel enough self-worth and satisfaction to avoid becoming a repeater. This esteem building will also enable her to improve her judgment; to feel better about herself; to find more viable solutions to her problems other than sexual."

Preparing a young woman for the grief she will experience is so important.

"Some girls will be so settled on adoption beforehand that they will avoid any bonding with their baby, and in some cases refuse to accept the identity of the child or an awareness of the animate person within them. Some people feel that if a woman cannot personify the embryo within them, then it is grounds for abortion. Unless a person's feelings are completely deadened, feelings arise naturally when the fetus or child leaves the womb. They may have accepted abortion or the adoption beforehand, but this can change when the baby leaves the birth canal.

When the child is finally born, guilt and shock may arise. Guilt because they considered giving the baby away, and shock because they never thought they would feel this way. "It can't be natural." "I must keep mv baby." "No one else could possibly take care of him like me." "How could I ever have considered giving him up?" Whereas they had anticipated the grief logically and to some degree emotionally, they are suddenly overwhelmed with feelings they were not supposed to experience."

When this grieving occurs, and it may begin even before the hospital stay, you need to let her know you care. Tell her that you would take that pain away in two seconds if you could. Let her know that is not possible for you to take away her pain, but you are going to walk through it with her.

The Dedication Service

We have found that many young woman are blessed by a dedication service in the hospital or before the adoption is final. This is a time of prayer with the people she feels closest to. This may include your family, her family, the counselor, her pastor, etc. Tom Dodge, in his article, "Good Adoption," describes this service so well.

"A prayer which best fits the feelings of that moment, fully expressive of the needs of the mother, is appropriate. There are no rituals in adoption other than the legal aspects, and yet the biological mother grieves like any other parent who has lost a child in death. What makes this situation so difficult is that the mother is choosing to separate in the best interest of her child. This is reminiscent of the Scripture account of the mother of the child who prevented Solomon from dividing her child in two pieces in I Kings 3. This woman loved her child and was willing to relinquish her child to the other woman in order to save his life. The biological mother is about to do the same. The dynamics of this situation must be understood. A compassionate God Who accepts the sorrow of His sheep and Who is a source of help and strength in a time of intense grief needs to be introduced. This is a time when the Christian faith can become a resource in the mourning which is about to follow, or is already manifesting itself.

"The following prayer might be offered:

"Precious Jesus, please hear us as we pour out our hearts to You. We know You love us and that as we cry You are

134

holding us in your warmth and compassion. Lord, we draw near to You for strength and help in our hour of pain.

"We thank You for the days we have had this child. She is so sweet and tender and a true product of Your loving grace. Protect her, dear Father. In the days ahead watch over, protect her, and lead her into Your righteousness.

"Jesus, now come with your blessings on (baby's name). Grant her peace which surpasses all understanding which only You can give. Watch over her and guide her in future days. Dear Jesus, thank You for hearing us and for being our comfort. Amen."

13

Saying Good-Bye

Since Mary entered our lives in 1972, many other young women have come to live with us and moved on. With each hello there has been a good-bye. Some of these good-byes have been very hard on our family, while others have been gratefully received! After saying good-bye, a time of loss always follows, no matter what type of relationship we had.

For the ones who were difficult, I am glad I reached out and did the best I could. For the ones who left out of rebelliousness or defiance, I grieve, because I know God wanted to do a work in them and they chose to say "no." For the ones who brought me joy, I have many wonderful memories. Many are still part of our lives today.

There is a time for moving on in all our lives, but it is so important that we know when that time is. The counselor and your pastor can be great helps during those times when you are not sure whether you should begin to help a young woman move towards leaving your home or not. John the Baptist was one who had a grasp on the principle of knowing when it was time to let go:

He (Jesus) must increase, but I must decrease. (John 3:30)

We must remember that these women are only a part of our families temporarily and were never meant to become permanent members. There are very few exceptions to this. Jim and I have lived with over 200 young women and today we have only three whom we consider as members of our family.

When the time comes to say good-bye, it is your responsibility to give her an idea of what type of contact with you would be appropriate:

Are you going to call her for lunch sometime, or should she call you to get together?

Are you going to say, "Write to me and I will write back," or vice versa?

Do you want to call her, or should she call you?

There are no right and wrong answers to these questions: they can go either way, depending on the relationship you feel you want to have with her. Just make sure you have clearly thought through your feelings and desires about continued contact.

Another point to remember is that just because you have said you would like to have continued contact with her, it does not necessarily mean she will desire the same kind of contact. If you call or write and she does not respond, do not push the relationship, but release it to the Lord. You were meant to be part of her life for a season, but as in so many relationships, she is moving on. You probably did a wonderful job and had a good relationship with her, but now that time is completed.

We can apply these principles to our lives with our children as well. How often we need to let go and to let them grow and learn on their own! Our relationships change as the years go by, but as we are able to release the old, God provides a new and better relationship for us.

There is often the question about what to do with the young woman whom you feel should leave, but has nowhere to go.

Before you take a young woman into your home, you should

know what the future holds for her, as much as possible. Will she be able to return home after her baby is born? Does she have other family members she is planning to live with? Is marriage in her future? Why does she need housing and for how long?

Even though it is true that the best plan can fall apart, at least you know what her resources are at the time she arrives at your door.

If she does not have any resources to begin with, you know she may require a longer stay, and you can assess whether you want your family to make this type of commitment.

If she comes close to delivering her baby and it is obvious she has no place to go, you and her counselor need to work together to discover all her possible resources.

Don't make staying in your home long-term too easy for her. From the beginning, you should state how long she may stay. Do *not* change that unless the circumstances are exceptional and her counselor is in agreement. We have found that many young women will say they have nowhere to go when, in reality, if you do not back down on your original plan, they will find a place to live.

If you need resources, sometimes the YWCAs or similar programs have rooms for rent. There are various women's shelters which will house women up to thirty days, and sometimes very small efficiency apartments or a room in someone's home can be rented at a small cost.

There is no question that there are no easy answers when this situation comes up. We often want the young woman to have an ideal setting to return to, but the reality is that few will accomplish this. Ultimately, it is the responsibility of the ministry or organization you are working with to find her a place to live. Your role is to love, pray, and know when to let go.

As each young woman leaves, it is good to have a time of sharing as a family. Allow the family to talk about the good and bad. Allow them to grieve.

Judy was a very special person in our lives. She had never been very difficult and she fit into our family almost immediately. Our family loves to play games and so did Judy. Judy had a sense of humor and had a special love for children. She was very good with both our girls. Each week she and our oldest daughter Holly would sit in a big overstuffed living room chair together and watch their favorite TV show. It was a special time for them.

As Judy's pregnancy progressed there was less and less room in the chair for Holly, but right up to the delivery date the two girls managed to get into that one chair! Then the time came for Judy to deliver her baby, and a little later, to leave us.

After Judy left our home, the night came for Holly's favorite show. Sensing her feeling of loss, I asked her if she would like for me to sit in the chair with her? "No, thanks, mom, I think I'll sit somewhere else tonight." As long as we had that chair, Holly rarely ever sat in it to watch television. A special thing had taken place in her life and she wanted to hold onto it in her own way. Judy and Holly still see each other from time to time. Holly is grown now, but they almost always mention this as a memorable time for both of them.

I am grateful that my children have learned how to care and how to love. I am grateful that they have learned not to run from pain, but to walk through it. There have been times of laughter and joy for us as young women have come into our lives. Deep lasting friendships have been formed and are still alive today.

Would I raise my children in the extended family setting if I had it to do all over again? Do I have regrets? Has my faith and trust in God increased because of this walk with Him? The answer to all these questions is yes. My regrets are the same as they are for every parent in the world. We are not perfect and we do make mistakes. One mistake we didn't make was having our family live unto itself.

"then the righteous will answer Him. 'Lord when did we see You hungry and feed You, or

140

thirsty and give You something to drink? When did we see You a stranger and invite You in, or needing clothes and clothe You?' The King will reply 'I tell you the truth, whatever you did for one of the least of these brothers of mine, you did for me.'" (Matt. 25:37,38,40)

Family Helps and Hints

We are looking forward to sharing our home. In order for our household to have order and to run smoothly we have established the following rules:

HOUSEKEEPING

1. You will participate in the daily tasks of housekeeping, cooking, laundry, etc.
2. Your bed shall be made by 10:00 AM
3. You will do your own laundry, including your towels and sheets. We do ask that you try to have a full machine. If the washing machine is not full, please ask to see if there are a few additional items that could be added from the general household.

GENERAL

1. Bedtime is 11:00 PM unless special permission is given.
2. Wake up time is 8:30 AM unless special permission is given. You are to be dressed and ready for the day by 10:00 AM
3. If you are going to be in your nightgown in the evening or in the morning before 10:00 AM you must wear a

robe. You are not allowed to get into your nightgown in the evening before 7:00 PM

4. We eat dinner together as a family. You will have some responsibility in meal planning and preparation.
5. We eat what is set before us unless there are special medical needs. As a family, we try to vary our meals to allow for everyone's favorites from time to time.
6. We bathe and shower daily, but are careful about the use of water.
7. You will not be allowed to drive our cars.
8. Lying will not be allowed.

MEDICAL

1. If you are caught with alcoholic beverages, or using or possessing drugs not prescribed by your physician, you shall be asked to leave our home within twenty-four hours.
2. Smoking is prohibited while at our home. This rule shall be observed by all members of your family and their visitors. The first offense shall receive a warning, second offense will have dishes for a week, third offense will have dishes for two weeks. A fourth offense is a decision to leave our home.
3. You shall attend childbirth classes, go to doctors' appointments, and follow their recommendations.

RELIGION

1. You will attend church with us or attend a Christian church in our community on Sunday mornings.
2. You shall have the opportunity to participate in other church activities and services in the community.
3. Blessing will be said at each meal.
4. You will be required to attend family devotions.

VISITATION

1. Your parents are welcome in our home with the understanding that they will notify us twenty-four hours in advance and work out arrangements for the visit with us.
2. Other relatives and friends will be allowed to visit on the same basis as parents. If your parents have an objection to a visitor, this will be given serious consideration on our part.
3. Boyfriends will not be allowed in our home in the absence of the foster father.
4. You will not be allowed to go out with friends and/or relatives without our approval.
5. Visits home shall be arranged with us. These visits shall not occur more than twice monthly or until you have been in our home for three weeks. Also, once visiting arrangements have been made, *they may not be changed*, in the middle of a visit except for extreme circumstances.
6. You will not be allowed to stay out all night with anyone other than your parents unless special permission is given.
7. No boyfriends shall be allowed Monday through Thursday during the school year, if you are in school or studying towards your high school equivalency test. Otherwise, boy-friends will be allowed to visit at our discretion.
8. Dating will be regulated and arranged according to your situation, and your parents' and our approval.

SCHOOL

1. If you have not graduated from high school, you shall attend school or study towards your high school equivalency test.

2. You shall be allowed to participate in any school-sponsored activity according to your physical ability and if your grades are average or above.
3. If you are maintaining below an average grade in any school subject, you shall be required to attend study hall for the remainder of the marking period and/or until the grade is raised to average or better. Study hall shall be held at the dining room table and shall consist of one hour per subject per day, except Saturday and Sunday.

PHONE

1. You shall be allowed to talk on the phone for fifteen (15) minutes. You must ask permission to make phone calls.
2. No phone calls shall be made in or out after 10:00 PM
3. Collect calls will not be accepted unless we give special permission.
4. You will not be allowed to call boys, but they are welcome to call you.
5. You will be responsible for paying all long distance phone calls which you make.

Misuse of any of these phone rules shall result in the following discipline:

First offense will receive a warning and the rule explained. Second and ongoing offenses will be given three days of phone restriction for each offense. No calls in or out, except for family contacts which will be limited to ten (10) minutes during the time of discipline.

TELEVISION, TAPE PLAYERS, RADIOS, STEREOS

1. All radios, stereos, tape players, etc. are to be off from 12:00 midnight to 9:00 AM

2. If your stereo, radio or tape player is found playing in an empty room, it will be confiscated for three days.
3. No television shall be allowed in your bedroom.
4. Stations, volume and time of listening are at our discretion. No earphones are allowed. Misuse of this privilege will result in confiscation of the radio, stereo, or tape player for one (1) week.
5. Records and tapes shall not be brought into our home without our approval.
6. Television shall be turned on only during the hours of 5:00 PM to 11:00 PM on Monday through Friday (except by special permission). On Sunday the television may be turned on after morning church service and remain on until 11:00 PM Television may be monitored by us. Misuse of this privilege will mean the loss of television privileges for one (1) week.

Name _____

WHAT I LIKE TO DO,
 WHAT I CAN DO WELL,
  WHAT I WISH I COULD DO BETTER:
1. Put a check next to those jobs you have done before:

Make a bed from scratch _____   Scrub the kitchen floor _____
Run a vacuum cleaner _____   Cut the grass _____
Scour a tub or toilet _____   Burn trash _____
Clean a refrigerator _____   Plan a menu _____
Do the laundry: Make a breakfast _____
  sort _____   Bake a cake _____
  wash _____   Wash a car _____
  dry _____   Work with farm animals _____
  fold and iron _____
2. How would you rate yourself in cooking ability?

    a. I still can't figure out how to turn the stove on.

b. I turn out a mean peanut-butter-and-jelly sandwich.
c. I feel confident making a few things, as long as I have a recipe.
d. Just call me Betty Crocker and point me to the kitchen.

3. Put a check () next to the items you have done before:

a. baked a cake from a box mix _____
b. baked a cake from scratch _____
c. made a breakfast _____
d. planned a dinner meal _____
e. done a week's grocery shopping with someone _____
f. done a week's grocery shopping alone _____
g. used coupons in a store _____
h. cooked an entire dinner meal alone _____
i. baked cookies _____
j. baked a pie _____

4. Name your favorite foods:

Cereals   Vegetables/Salads   Meats   Desserts   Other

5. What foods do you like for breakfast?

6. What would be your favorite dinner if you could have anything?

    Meat:
    Vegetables/Salad:
    Dessert:

7. What foods don't you like at all?

8. What are your present hobbies? _____

_____

Past hobbies? (if different from today) _____

_____

9. Do you participate in sports? _____

Sing? _____   Draw or paint? _____
Write? _____   Dance? _____
10. Play a musical instrument? _____
11. Would you rather be a spectator or a player of sports
events? _____

_____

12. What activity do you enjoy more than anything else? _____

_____

13. What activities do you wish you had more time and/or
money to do? _____

_____

14. How do you feel about these crafts and hobbies?

	Have done	Would like to do	No thanks
Puzzle Craft			
Jewelry-making			
Candle-making			
Needlework:			
Crewel			
Embroidery			
Needlepoint			
Cross Stitch			
Knitting			
Crocheting			
Collage			
Painting			
Macrame			
Silk Screening			
Finger Painting			

Weaving _____

String Art _____

Sewing _____

Cooking _____

Others: _____

_____

_____

15. Is there anything more you'd like to do? _____

_____

16. How well do you like school? _____

_____

17. How many years have you attended school? _____

_____

18. What subjects do you:

Like very much _____

Dislike very much _____

Need help with _____

19. What further education do you plan? _____

20. Has school been:

       (a)easy   (b)difficult

       (c)fairly easy   (d)very difficult

21. In what extracurricular activities have you been involved?

_____

_____

_____

22. Do you enjoy reading? _____

What magazines do you read on a regular basis? _____

_____

If you had the time, what books would you read? _____

_____

Book List

The following are books that deal with sexuality, teenage pregnancy, parents, and parenting. We highly recommend them for your information. Some of them are appropriate for young women and would be ideal reading material to keep on hand in your homes. Most of these books are available from your local Christian bookstore, or can be ordered from:

Loving and Caring
100 Foxshire Drive
Lancaster, PA 17601

Abortion and Healing	Michael T. Mannion, Sheed & Ward
Amen	Keith Yoder
Bittersweet	Gay Lewis, Bridge Publishing Co.
Caring Enough to Confront	David Augsberger, Regal Books
The Caring Father	Wilson Wayne Grant, MD, Broadman Press
A Case for Adoption	Cheryl Kreykes Brandsen Bethany Christian Services
Five Cries of Youth	Merton Strommen Harper & Row
Five Cries of Parents	Merton Strommen Harper & Row
Givers, Takers and Other Kinds of Lovers	Josh McDowell, Living Books

How To Really Love Your Child	Ross Campbell, Victor Books
How to Really Love Your Teenager	Ross Campbell Victor Books
The Hurting Parent	Margie Lewis Zondervan Books
I Gave God Time	Ann Kiemel Anderson Tyndale House Publishers
I Loved a Girl	Walter Trobisch
If God Loves Me, Why Can't I Get My Locker Open?	Lorraine Peterson Bethany House Publishers
I'm Running to Win	Ann Kiemel Anderson Tyndale House Publishers
Just Like Ice Cream	Lissa Halls Johnson Bantam Books
Lisa	Betty Shaffer Bethany House Publishers
Looking for Love in All the Wrong Places The Missing Piece	Joe White Lee Ezell Harvest House
Mom, I'm Pregnant	Bev O'Brien Tyndale House Publishers
Ordering Your Private World	Gordon McDonald Oliver Nelson Books
Radical Hospitality	David and Ruth Rupprecht Presbyterian & Reformed Publishing Company

Seven Styles of Parenting	Pat Hershey Owen, Tyndale House Publishers
Should I Keep My Baby?	Martha Zimmerman, Bethany House Publishers
Straightforward	Larry Tomczak, Logos International
Struggling for Wholeness	Ann Kiemel Anderson and Jan Kiemel Ream, Oliver Nelson Books
Teens Parenting	Jeanne Warren Lindsay, Morning Glory Press
Taste of Tears, Touch of God	Ann Kiemel Anderson, Oliver Nelson Books
Who Broke the Baby?	Jean Garton, Bethany House Publishers
Why Was I Adopted?	Carole Livingstone, Lyle Stuart, Inc.
Winterflight	John Bayly, Word Books
Your Attitude Key to Success	John C. Maxwell, Here's Life Publishers

Work List

THE DAILY GRIND:

Laundry _____
Collect clothes baskets from each room. Take to laundry.
Collect bath and dish towels.
Supervise machines and/or line dry.
Sort and fold clothes and deliver to rooms.

Bathrooms _____
Clean toilets, tubs, tile walls, sinks, soapdishes.
Clean mirrors.
Check supplies: toilet paper (get more from storage if needed).
Floors washed Mon., Wed., Fri.
Put out clean towels & washclothes.

Chefs of the Day
1. Cook _____
2. Helper:
   Make a dessert, if desired.
   Feed animals — 4:00.
   Set table; prepare beverages — juice, water, milk.
   Prepare & serve tea or coffee.
   Serve dessert. _____

ENVIRONMENTAL CONCERNS

Dishpan Hands Department
Includes: sweeping floor after each meal; scouring sink, counter top & stove surface (check burner drip pans). Wash tablecloth.
BR _____
LN _____
DN _____

Evening Clean-up _____
Wash Dishes.
Scour kitchen sink & counter tops, sweep floors, wash tablecloth.
Straighten living room.

Upstairs Cleaning
Yellow room _____
Betsy & Tom's room _____
Blue room _____
Hall, linen closet, stairs _____

First Floor Cleaning
Living room _____
Green room _____
Hallway _____
Boys office/pantry _____

Basement
Recreation room _____
Laundry Area _____

154

Work List continued

SOME LIKE IT FRESH: CHANGING SHEETS

Strip beds and deliver sheets to laundry room. Each person gets own fresh sheets and makes bed.

Yellow room   Tues._____

Blue room   Wed._____

Kevin & Owen   Thurs._____

Tom & Betsy   Fri. _____

Guest bed   _____

SPOT CHECKS: STITCHES-IN-TIME:

_____Wash kitchen floor.

_____Wash and wax kitchen floor.

_____Wash windows _____ room.

_____ Sweep porch.

_____ Sweep steps leading to outside cellar door.

_____Clean and resort cupboards

    Kitchen _____
    Pantry _____
    Linen _____

_____Empty wastebaskets.

_____Water plants.

_____Clean out refrigerator; wash top & fingerprints on door.

_____Clean oven.

_____Outside jobs: _____
    _____
    _____

DUSTER'S DELIGHT

FAMILY & DINING ROOM _____
HALL & STAIRS _____

ALL THAT TRASH

COLLECT TRASH _____
BURN TRASH _____

FLOORS GALORE

KITCHEN FLOOR _____
PANTRY _____
PANTRY FLOOR _____
FOYER _____

FRIDGE & OVEN

CLEAN FRIDGE _____
CLEAN OVEN _____

TUBS & TILES

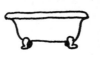

DOWNSTAIRS BATHROOM _____
UPSTAIRS BATHROOM _____
ANNE & JIM'S BATHROOM _____

LOADS OF FUN...

LAUNDRY _____
LAUNDRY ROOM _____

LES BOUDOIRS

A & J'S ROOM _____
HOLLY'S ROOM _____
SHELLY'S ROOM _____
BARB'S ROOM _____
MARG'S ROOM _____
CONNIE'S ROOM _____

THIRSTY PLANTS

WATER PLANTS _____